T0152826

Death Watch

Gerald Stern

Death Watch

A VIEW FROM THE TENTH DECADE

Trinity University Press | SAN ANTONIO

Published by Trinity University Press
San Antonio, Texas 78212

Copyright © 2017 by Gerald Stern

All rights reserved. No part of this book may be reproduced in
any form or by any electronic or mechanical means, including
information storage and retrieval systems, without permission in
writing from the publisher.

Cover design by Rebecca Lown
Book design by BookMatters
Cover art: istock/pegasophoto

ISBN 978-1-59534-784-8 paper
ISBN 978-1-59534-785-5 ebook

Trinity University Press strives to produce its books using
methods and materials in an environmentally sensitive manner.
We favor working with manufacturers that practice sustainable
management of all natural resources, produce paper using
recycled stock, and manage forests with the best possible
practices for people, biodiversity, and sustainability. The press
is a member of the Green Press Initiative, a nonprofit program
dedicated to supporting publishers in their efforts to reduce
their impacts on endangered forests, climate change, and forest-
dependent communities.

The paper used in this publication meets the minimum
requirements of the American National Standard for
Information Sciences—Permanence of Paper for Printed Library
Materials, ANSI 39.48—1992.

CIP data on file at the Library of Congress

21   20   19   18   17 | 5   4   3   2   1

Contents

Preface

I am saying to myself that I'm writing about a final journey. But it seems too ridiculously pompous and sentimental. It makes me think of Tom Mix or Gene Autry riding a piebald into the mountains at sunset, the strings playing "I'm Heading for the Last Roundup," which unfortunately I know all the words to. Maybe all lives don't end in the casting away of the trivial and a clinging, an adherence to one thing, a place, a memory, an act, maybe a certain garden or a strong beam in an attic or a back porch over which the rope will be flung, but in the unanswered questions, the ones that William James asked no one, for no one was his god. In my case, what I should read in the short space of time remaining to me, where I should be buried, what I should decide—if the choice is given to me—to remember, what I should do about being a Jew, what I should teach my grandchildren, if I'm given the opportunity, should I adhere more to truth than to fiction, what the difference is, if my own life had any significance among the billions and billions more to come, what I should celebrate. Certainly there'll be a graveyard or two, a lot of hills, rivers, meadows—with daisies—pine trees, smoke and fog, tried and true radicals, donkeys, dogs; some sad love, four or five great cities, celebrations, encounters, jails, books, a lot of childhood, forgotten heroes and heroines, some failures, some victories, (small and not so small), a bit of philosophy, and a bit of repetition and, since it is death we're talking about, some decomposition and gruesomeness; and friends, always friends—and neighbors. Friends and neighbors. For I have befriended many, migrant that I am, and beneighbored even more. And I will please you, I hope, by not ever saying, here or elsewhere, either "god bless," or "enjoy."

Jacob

Every once in a while—at an odd or unexpected time—I think of my Hebrew name and what I'm called in English and how I hate what came down and what the permutations, complications, and connections are. If your name is Yaakov—or Ya'agobh—it should be Jacob, but the Americanized Jewish mothers were allowed to stray as long as they were true to the initial (harsh) sound. Thus, it could be Jerome, or Jack, or James, or Gerald. I even know someone, born in Germany, whose name is "Gerd," the male form of "Gerda," he told me, but when I asked what his Hebrew name was he said Yaakov, so he was Jacob too. Of course, I had to first ascertain that he was Jewish. His last name is the same as mine, so he could be German or even English, but when he told me he was born in Germany and his family left in 1936, I knew he was a Yidl, even if his father, who, he told me, hated Polish Jews because they were dirty, discovered to his horror, slow-witted as he was, that

Germans didn't like Jews, Polish *or* German, even if they had raised, trained, and sold horses to the German army for a hundred years or more. This same father drove Gerd into a mental institution in New York, the very same one Karl Solomon (of *Howl*) and Allen Ginsberg were guests in and all at the very same time. Of course my own family's last name only became "Stern" at Ellis Island, the second year of the twentieth century. It was some godforsaken unpronounceable Ukrainian name before that, not suitable among Anglo-Saxons.

Jacob, you may remember, is clever, deceitful, blasphemous, a kind of thief and a purveyor of fraud. Above all, he is a liar. More cunning than clever. A con artist, yet one of the three patriarchs. He was settled, orderly, and intelligent, a cross between a lawyer and a wrestler. And a favorite of his mother; compared to his brother, hairless. He struggled constantly to obtain his hungry brother Esau's birthright (for a plate of noodles); to get blind Isaac's blessing (through pretense); to marry his cousin, Rachel; to make peace with Esau; to defeat "a man" in an all-night wrestling match and to insist that "the man" bless him and change his name to "Israel," not, you might say, the function of a wrestler or even an angel—as he is commonly seen—but of Grandfather Divine himself, changer of names and maker of nations. He—Jacob—reminds me a good deal of Odysseus, who is also cunning, full of tricks, and a survivor. He could have been a favorite type of hero for that early world, not purely ethical, as we later preferred our heroes, but probably more in sync with the ideal mode of warrior behavior among shepherds and such. High (anthropological) criticism in the late nineteenth century tended to socialize individual actions, and, as such, the behavior of such a "hero" as Jacob, in his relations with his uncle (and father-in-law) and twin brother, Esau, were seen as allegories of social dynamic and social change such as the movement away from hunting to agriculture, urbanism, and trade. When the grand Jewish heroes, prophets, and saints came along, they were not "representative" but stood on their own big feet and spoke with their own fat lips.

Why I wanted to be a Jacob in the first place or, at a minimum, loyal to his memory, since I was blessed with his name (as was my paternal grandfather and five of my male cousins, two Jeromes, two Jacks, and a Gerard, but no [other] Gerald), is peculiar, given the history; but it may have had something to do with dumb loyalty, on the one hand, or just rejection of the substitute name, a sissy name in my youth, to my ears like "Percy" or "Sidney,"

little better than Henry or Arnold. Gerald is Teutonic
and it means "spear-wielder," whereas my only spear was
a well-sharpened pencil, besides which I intensely disliked
the very sound of "Gerald." Give me Jacob any day, even if
I didn't cheat my father, outwit my brother, and wrestle
with God. A little wrestling maybe but no twin brother,
only a sister who died when she was nine—and I eight.
Sylvia, common enough, since names come and go in
aggregates, or maybe there was an actress. No "person"
as I remember; no Hebrew to speak of. In my own life,
I was actually more than a little Jacobean. I organized,
ministered, led, negotiated, outwitted. Some of the things
I did, which required the example of a wily Jacob or Odysseus, was to organize and lead marches as part of the Civil
Rights movement; negotiate contracts (AFT) and lead (suc-
cessful) strikes; amass a whole body of poets (forty, I remember) to teach Poetry-in-the-Schools in Pennsylvania,
and train and evaluate them in all sixty-three counties;
to organize my own defense—at the last minute—when
I was subject to a major court-martial just after World
War II; and to organize a veritable army to combat—*and
end*—violence against Jewish students in my high school
in Pittsburgh (when I was a sophomore), home of three
rivers and twenty kinds of hatred. Either Yaakov or Odys-

seus would have been a good debater on our college debate team where we never lost one debate; not to mention that writing itself requires the brain of a Jacob and the moves of an Odysseus. My name in the old country would have been Yunkel, which is Yiddish for Jacob.

Trip to Kehilat HaNahar Synagogue

I was a little bit stuck on the small bridge that separates New Jersey from Pennsylvania, Lambertville from New Hope, when I thought of some of this. Though it was confusing when the river itself, below the bridge, came into view, rain peppering it, a small mist rising, trees and hills in the distance unbearably beautiful, the next bridge, a mile north, peaceful and beckoning. It may have been rush hour. The month was July. I was on my way, in the heavy rain, to the Reconstructionist Synagogue in New Hope, just out of curiosity sort of, for I had only been there once and I wasn't altogether sure of the route. I had been interested—sort of—in this branch of Judaism for the last twenty years; it was the only one that elicited any kind of emotional response from me—though not enough to attend services, Friday night *or* Saturday. The one time I had been there was at the invitation of the former rabbi,

Sandy Parrian, to participate in a small study group that met weekly to examine biblical questions, to argue I discovered, peacefully among themselves, over issues fairly far removed from their diurnal concerns. I guess it was Talmudic; maybe more Midrashic. I think I was vaguely on the way to meet the new rabbi, also a woman and a Reconstructionist. Maybe I would open the front door and walk in, though it was a fool's errand since it was six o'clock in the evening and there was not likely to be anyone there. I was practicing.

I was friends with Sandy. I met her on a street corner shortly after moving to Lambertville from Iowa. She was talking to an old friend of mine who happened to die a few weeks later. I did a sort of dance and recited a poem—Yeats, I think—and when I discovered she was a rabbi, I started to sing bruchas. It was astonishingly stupid, but she rode above it, as it were, and we made a date to have lunch the next week. Anne Marie says that I always had a thing for her, which might be true. At any rate we met every few weeks to talk about books, family, and such. I was in my seventies and half thinking of where I should be buried, so we spent some time looking at graveyards. I'm in my late eighties now and still haven't decided. Maybe I think that will stall the Malachamavet, angel of death. It could be that's why I was driving to the synagogue, in the heavy rain, the first week of July 2013.

I did meet someone at the front door of the synagogue, but it wasn't the rabbi. It was the camp director of the camp they ran in and around the building—very pastoral. She had a large green umbrella and looked at my car for a few seconds, not, I think, suspiciously though the synagogue is up a very steep driveway, more or less in some woods and very isolated. As she came over I opened my window and talked to her. I asked her what time Friday-night services were and such. She seemed to trust me, maybe because I dropped a few Yiddish words. On the way back down, really when I got to the light, I decided to make a left turn and go up the river on the Pennsylvania side instead of crossing the New Hope bridge again into Lambertville. The whole stretch along the river there (Route 32) is gorgeous. The road takes sharp turns, steep hills on the left, the Pennsylvania Canal, then the Delaware River on the right, sometimes enormous mansions on the river side, then—through the little villages—old stone houses directly on the road, on both sides. I have traveled it up and down for years and I know most of the restaurants, hotels, and stores. I crossed to the Jersey side on the Frenchtown Bridge and traveled south on the quick road back to Lambertville. The name of the synagogue is Kehilat HaNahar (the Little Shul by the River), and the rabbi's name is Diana Miller.

In the meantime, I carried on with my reading, for I always do that, rain or shine. In the last five or six months, I have been reading fiction—or pseudofiction—vaguely in preparation or as a corollary to what I'm doing now, Blaise Cendrars, Sebald, Céline, Genet, Henry Miller. It's not that I like them all. Some of it is boring, distasteful, and wearying. But I'm in the trenches and I carry on, fleas, mud, freezing cold, blazing heat, phone calls, letters, requests, stupid journals, backache, whatnot. What I hate in particular are certain memoirs. Those that center on abuse and redemption, or even worse, confessions of "sinful acts" and the cure via religion, mountain-climbing, charity, voluntary poverty, or deep breathing and self-congratulation. We love to confess to each other, we Catholics manqués, and nothing is beyond bounds, if you signify regret—and add remorse as a seasoning—variously including cannibalism, incest, animal mutilation, flag-burning, disrespect of corporations, wife-beating, wife-swapping, gun-clinging, racism, nihilism, filthy underwear, hatred of dwarves, hatred of Jews, old people, cats, monkeys, elephants, the poor, the meek, the helpless, orphans, widows, moles, molasses, Heinz ketchup, Hellman's mayonnaise, and dog shit. These days I am rereading Céline, his *Journey to the End of the Night*, plus Milton Hindus's *Céline: The Crippled Giant*, an intensive correspondence as well as commentary, an introduction (actually two), and an afterword. Hindus was a college professor (Chicago, Brandeis), a Jew, and a great admirer of Céline's "fiction." The correspondence shows real affection between the two, and Hindus actually made a trip to Denmark to see Céline (where he was exiled and imprisoned). They both close their letters with salutations like "Affectionately Yours" and "Your Good Friend." When they met, things rather fell apart. Almost at once. Later, when Hindus published his book on Céline, Céline, in spite of the hard evidence, denied they had written each other or met in Denmark. He actually wrote a book entitled *Conversations with Professor Y* (Yid?) in 1955, full of satire, denial, and ridicule. Céline wrote a series of vicious "anti-Semitic" pamphlets in the late 1930s that rather aligned him on the side of the Nazis, the collaborationists, and old-school Jew-haters. He never apologized in the correspondence—but made vague cryptic remarks more expressing his self-pity than his regret. "Oh, I assure you that I am cured of the desire to worry over things that don't concern me" is as far as he went. He was cunning, evasive, blustering, and bastardly. He spoke to French slave laborers in Germany at the invitation of Dr. Goebbels and fled France—in 1944—with the German army. But in his letters to Hindus he belittles Hitler and the Nazi enterprise. Hindus had the mind-set of an English professor. He excused poets from their crimes— as if they were entitled to a different standard of moral behavior (Pound, Byron). Although in his final evaluation Hindus speaks with a different voice and recognizes Louis Destouches (Céline) for what he was, a magnificent writer but a goddamn fool.

I called it pseudofiction since it is more in the way of "mere" prose narrative than traditional novel. Sebald called it prose fiction and refused the designation of novelist. I have read and reread much of Genet, including *Our Lady of the Flowers* and *Miracle of the Rose*. Genet is described as a novelist and listed that way by Gallimard, but it's mostly untransformed autobiography. I say "untransformed" and that's the key. Fiction, whatever it is, seems to want a trajectory, and the presence of what you might call a secret, especially an unspoken one, and a mystery of sorts. Something besides merely an author. Reading Cendrars, for example, is like reading—or having read to you—an endless letter of someone's travels and adventures, in Russia, China, and Brazil. The fact that the author lies or exaggerates does not turn it into a novel. Not as such. Our Miller—who wrote about Miller, though sometimes Miller in Greece and sometimes Miller in New York—is constantly being reevaluated. I think he is best read when you're under thirty—I even want to say twenty-three—later he seems too pompous, opinionated, repetitive, and predictable. He is not D. H. Lawrence. But I am beginning now to appreciate what sinks to the bottom—I should say rises to the top—and stays there. His testimony, some of it, much of it, certainly not none of it, is worth keeping. Sebald I am reading from a different perspective than I did ten years ago. At his best, at his worst, he moves freely from place to place, from thought to thought and book to book and obscure philosopher to more obscure planetologist or librarian in a more or less unpredictable way—though it's not a familiar narrative—rather a kind of scientific or philological voyage or treatise or travelogue that is never ending since, although there is a kind of beginning, there is really no end. Thus it's, at least to him, a giant metaphor for life itself—well, human life—and if you follow him, and accept him, you find existence verbalized in some mysterious manner. I love everything he's written, from *Rings of Saturn*—which typifies his fragmented style—to *Austerlitz*, which is really—finally—a true novel. Well, almost. He is a master of the decayed, abandoned, and destroyed, especially in *Rings of Saturn*. There he writes about the silkworm industry in Europe, the carpet bombing of German cities, old resorts, neglected gardens, the Edict of Nantes, and the first performance of Handel's *Messiah*—in that order. He is part bitter, part sad about Germany, and feels cheated of his life, as other Germans I have met who were born just at the end of, or just after, the war.

Austerlitz is a novel concerning *kinder transport*, specifically about a lost soul who was adopted by a Methodist minister (from Wales) and his wife who never told him what his family name was or that he was Jewish, and the book—*Austerlitz*—is his liberating, but deeply sad, discovery of these facts. My favorite book of Sebald's is *The Emigrants*, a book about four Germans in exile and where their wanderings take them. I am most moved by the second narrative, that of Paul Bereyton, a devoted grade school teacher who, because he is one-quarter Jewish, is dismissed from his post, though being three-quarters Aryan, an absurd nomenclature at any rate, he is called up for service in the Wehrmacht and serves on many fronts— for six years in all—during the war. We know early that he kills himself by lying across train tracks, but the time leading up to that is related by a Madame Landau, a friend of Paul's (Sebald's way of doing things) who had arranged for his burial and whom the narrator—never named—is talking to. Paul, she said, was "almost consumed by the loneliness within him." She describes his move to Besançon, in France, as a tutor (following his dismissal), and his move after that to Berlin, a city he hardly knew, where he was conscripted. Madame Landau ends her long tale with observations of how much railroads—the smoke, the depots, the carriages—meant to Paul, even when he was young. Visiting his aunt and uncle, Paul, she said, was always late for dinner, causing his uncle to say, "You'll end up on the railways," certainly a "darkly foreboding" statement, Madame Landau observes. He apparently lay his glasses neatly down, certainly folded, before he stretched his body over the rails. He was going blind but was grateful, he said, for the time given him. I was moved at the end of this narrative more than by reading anything else—in years. Heartbreaking, true, quietly told. This primary school teacher exiled—and ruined—because he was a quarter Jewish, in a hopeless corner of Germany, near Switzerland.

David Shields, in *PEN America* (2012), has a kind

of manifesto or poem—on the subject of the novel—in thirty-nine sections. The last section reads: "After Freud, after Einstein, the novel retreated from narrative, poetry retreated from rhyme, and art retreated from the representative into the abstract." His statements reflect a lot of current thought on the subject: "the origin of the novel lies in its pretense of actuality" (4). "The word 'novel' when it entered the languages of Europe, had the vaguest of meaning; it meant the form of writing that was formless, that had no rules, that made its own rules as it went along" (26).

> The earliest use of writing was list-making for commercial transactions. (2)

> Storytelling can be traced back to Hindu sacred writings, known as the Vedas, around 1400 BC. (5)

> In seventeenth-century France, Madeleine de Scudéry (in Artamène) and Madame de Lafayette (in La Princesse de Clèves) wrote about the romantic intrigues of aristocrats. (19)

> The origin of the novel lies in its pretense of actuality. (24)

> In the eighteenth century, Defoe, Richardson, and Fielding overthrew the aristocratic romance by writing

fiction about a thief, a bed-hopper, and a hypocrite—
novels featuring verisimilitude, the unfolding of
individual experience over time, causality, character
development. (27)

In order to read *Finnegans Wake* (in 1946, two years
after Sebald was born), I locked myself in my parents'
apartment—they were in the Catskills—for a week, filled
the refrigerator, and read a given number of pages a day. I
still love the book. I am a memory-fiend, like Sebald. If I
went from place to place, from thought to thought, as he
did, I might write of early—and late—love, of the Haymarket Rebellion, of the Makhnovist Movement, an anarchist
rebellion in the early Soviet days, and I would retell and
enlarge upon my arrest (at Camp Holabird) and imprison-
ment in Aberdeen Proving Grounds in Maryland. Those
are the first four things that come to mind. Next week it
could be different. I hate the word "revisit" by the way; it's
one of the dumb words of our new technology. I also hate
the word "texting." I not only hate the *thing*, the ridiculous
activity, I hate the *word*. I guess there are prose books that
are not novels, or novel-like. Technical, critical, scientific.
A history book, maybe. In the novel there has to be cunning, tongue-in-cheek, hidden methodology. Every piece

of writing affirms, reaffirms, denies, changes, refines, challenges, bedevils, mocks, transforms, domesticates, radicalizes what came before. Fielding leads to Beckett; Richardson to Genet. I'm suddenly thinking of *The Enormous Room*, by Cummings. An extraordinary piece of prose that marks Cummings's total lack of faith, of belief, in any system whatsoever. It even explains his typography and orthography. For some uncanny reason I don't get tired of Céline's cynicism as I do of Henry Miller's. Genet overwhelms us with details (with truth); Edmund White's biography of Genet is superb. Blaise Cendrars is not only a "neo" novelist (or travel writer), he also wrote one of the two best poems in French in the twentieth century, "Les Pâques à New York." He was, when he wrote it, cold and starving. But it's a tender, beautifully rendered long poem, most of it written in the new library on Fifth Avenue (1910) where he went to stay warm. My problem now is to keep track of the books themselves, my reading—no easy matter.

Early Love

I think I was just twenty when I created my first domestic arrangement with a young woman, who had the same first name as I did only she spelled it Jerri, giving it a certain flair, making it almost French. We met, Jerri and I, at Pitt, where we were both students. I was majoring in political science and philosophy, and, as I recall, she was an English and French major. We met in what was called the Commons Room in that vertical schoolhouse called the Cathedral of Learning, and it had to be just after the war. She was a sex-worker, as it is now called, in the red-light district by the river on the north side, so romanticized by the Naturalists, and had her own small apartment nearby where she lived with her daughter—who was two or three at the time, watched over by her aunt. I remember her sitting at her rickety desk, eyeglasses far down on her nose, reading *Père Goriot*, Balzac on the Allegheny. By this time her French was good enough for her to read almost without utilizing the dictionary. She was quite beautiful, square shoulders, small breasts, full hips, long legs, soulful and unpretentious. She had a trusting face and a large smile. She was the grandchild or the great-grandchild of a cross between a manacled black slave from West Africa and a manacled white convict from England or Ireland. Her grandfather and grandmother, she told me, had walked from a town in southern Georgia north to Pittsburgh during the First World War to work in steel. Jerri had been raised on "The Hill" where I was born a year after her and where my grandparents settled after coming to this country from Poland and Ukraine. Certainly, they had not swum over the Atlantic as her grandparents had walked north, stopping, she told me, at African American churches along the way in towns all through the mountainous route, certainly with an address in Pittsburgh, a cousin or an uncle who would help them get settled—just as my grandparents had names and addresses, only written down in Yiddish, using, as it does, Hebrew characters. I used to try to talk to her about the deep connections between Jews and blacks, but she wasn't much interested in what she called "sociology." When I tried to talk to her about her work she wasn't very forthcoming. I sometimes peppered her with questions, but she shut me up in dif-

ferent ways, including putting a hand on my mouth, and
sometimes her lips. I spent long afternoons in her apartment reading and writing while she worked on her Balzac.
We took long walks past the large houses a few blocks up
where I'd climb onto the porches and look into the windows (nostalgic for what I never had) while she waited on
the sidewalk. I was fascinated by the turn-of-the-century—
and earlier—woodwork, staircases, and furniture. It was
already to me like a museum. What attracted me to her
was the exotic nature of her work (as I saw it), her little
girl, her more-or-less double life, our peaceful and relaxed
sex life, and most of all, the fact that she had a separate
and self-determined existence, a kind of mission and lived
(as I saw it) in a kind of mystery. She was autonomous
and carried her own burden. I admired this endlessly. It
was the thing that always moved me in a girlfriend—or
a wife. Her self-determined existence. Needless to say, I
never visited her at the place where she worked. It was on a
street where—on weekends late at night—cars were lined
up and city cops kept order. Periodically, the mayor would
come by with an ax and a photographer, but that was just
for publicity and to pull the curtains down on the eyeballs
of the sanctimonious middle classes, in all the boroughs

and across all the bridges of our dirt-ridden city. Dirt and dust; darkness and flames; our own hell.

We spent over a year together before my time in the army. I never thought of marriage—I had to go to Europe first, learn some languages, wear a beret. If couples break up, it's often, maybe always, over lack of sexual intimacy— that more than money. Jerri and I had amazing intimacy, shared fantasies, and were direct about our feelings. But one thing she wouldn't talk about was her sexual activity at work. I don't think she was ashamed of it—she just kept it to herself, or kept it away from me. We didn't have intimacy there. And we never would.

As far as jealousy, I accepted without reservation Jerri's distinction of "work" as opposed to pleasure, or satisfaction. It's a subtle point, and certainly can be seen so in some cases more than others, but I was too naïve, inexperienced—ignorant—to challenge the position. I was full of juices, but I didn't even have the imagination yet that would have made it possible for me to conceive of amatory details that might cause me agony—on the one hand—or perverse gratification on the other. I was a ridiculous romantic, ignorant of Blake and Byron, even if I were reading them already. There also had to be an

element of racism in my privileged position, especially in
my smug self-congratulation, such as it was, rising out of
my "generosity and lack of bigotry." Certainly there was a
Baudelarian effect in my idealization of the "Negress," but
I suspect I hadn't put things together enough even to be
knowledgeable of the similar concept, the "Jewess," I was
so uneducated, I lacked such cynicism, I was so out of it.
Or I just isolated the relationship out of all social considerations. I was a fool. With no regret and no bitterness.
Maybe no memory.

One day as I was questioning her about the intricacies
of her trade, the role of the Madame, male authority, the
arrogance of customers, the *culture* of the whorehouse,
and she saw I was taking notes, she angrily asked me if
I were writing about it, about her. When I confessed I
was writing a novel she became furious (and rightly so).
Nor could I blame Emile Zola or Frank Norris or Stephen
Crane for my behavior. "Get the fuck out," she said, "and
take your books and notebooks with you." It would most
likely have been one or two o'clock in the afternoon, and
that may have been the beginning of my first long walk,
followed through the years by many others, to go over the
words, to regret, to have remorse, to be amazed at my stu-
pidity, to decide what to do next, to relocate myself, to find

my balance, to be hopeful, to be destitute. I should have gone back, I should have apologized, but I never saw Jerri again, except distantly, in the Commons Room (on the first floor of the university), with its dark spaces and large wooden chairs and tables and giant chandeliers where she hung out with other black students, the few that were there, nor did she ever approach me, even to argue or accuse. I was devastated. I think if I had had sisters I might have known better how to behave, what to do. But, as it turned out, I was ignorance itself.

Last Journey

Piling up books—like towers in every inch of available space—was not much different fifty, sixty years ago than it is today, only the current crop is often whimsical, specialized, arrived at from God knows where, sometimes just dead-ended and finally senseless, or at least not of great consequence, though sometimes leading to a discovery—or itself a discovery—picked up from one of the selfsame towers that are exhibited on folding tables along Upper Broadway as they were once exhibited alongside the French river between the stone bridges where we walked and sometimes read our eyes out, a mere foot away from the impatient and observant purveyors, those eternal *bouquinistes.* Just a week ago I bought a book for seven dollars and fifty cents on Broadway (reduced from ten) called *History of the Makhnovist Movement, 1918–1921,* by one Peter Arshinov. Because it sounded insanely familiar and had—I somehow recollected—something to do with

my family though I'd have to figure it out on the red side
chair here in New York on 110th Street between Broadway
and Riverside (fourth floor). It is a digression, again, but
everything is digression. Life itself is grand digression—
you on your way to oblivion, the last supper not what you
think, either steak and ice cream, or a piece of raw broccoli
for your health's sake, in your chains and slippers, a rabbi
with an English accent beside you mumbling in Babylonian, both of you in a 1936 movie starring Paul Muni, on
your way to your last shelter and offering your small guests
your crossed hands and lips as you did once before only
on the upper side, or still arguing with yourself over the
question of methodology, still resisting the fire, for reasons beyond you. And what would be the good to consult
with this or that Diana except for the sake of a last decent
thing, to be among your own kind for once, though you
never were before, or rather yours was another altogether.
I'll talk to Rabbi Miller as I once did to Rabbi Parrian and
will compare one graveyard to another. Again. My big
sister and most of my relatives are on a crowded hill off
Route 51, in Pittsburgh; and my father and mother are side
by side in the tropics, near a rusted fence, garbage piled up
beside them. So I'm free—am I not? Though going down
about 10:30 this morning with my granddaughter Julie to

the Tot Lot on 112th and Riverside, where she swung and slid and climbed and jumped for about an hour, we saw at the nether end of a park bench a dead pigeon with his two eyes plucked out and a few torn feathers in their place, so soon, speaking of small guests, speaking of aboves and belows.

My second cousin, maybe a third depending on how—and when—you counted, had a government job interviewing refugees, mostly from Ukraine and Romania. He interviewed a Ukrainian Jew who was hoping to settle in Seattle, and after a few words he realized that he—the Ukrainian—had the same last name as he, more or less, since Ukrainian Jews take liberties, and that he may have been the grandson or great-grandson of my second cousin's own great-grandfather's brother, or perhaps *his* cousin. And what suddenly came to light was the distant memory of a self-proclaimed anarchist, out of the Jewish tradition, who may have been involved in that selfsame insurrection which my book, *History of the Makhnovist Movement*, describes, that took place in the southern Ukraine, a revolt mainly against the Bolsheviks who were already, even at that early date (1918), abandoning their first principles by establishing hierarchies and all the other paraphernalia of statecraft, jailing "enemies," shooting them, really creating an enemy class, which it continually did all through its long life, even—later—in Spain, even in the blocks surrounding Union Square near Klein's Tower, in the 1920s, '30s, and '40s, finally submitting, of all things, to a richer, more cunning, and better-armed enemy a continent away, laboring under fifty stars and a few stripes, adopting the other forms of greed and mostly abandoning the virtues it once had.

The Russian Empire was going crazy in the years before and during and after World War I, trying to make its mind up on what kind of madness could be imposed on a suffering and dreaming people, as all the theories were being worked out, in real time—with real blood. The anarchists who had been on the front line of revolution for decades were respected by, and made alliances with, the Reds and fought against the Whites in its various glosses, but were—finally—treated contemptuously (by the Bolsheviks) as mere, or misguided, theorists, incapable of social action, because such, they said, was basically contrary to their very beliefs.

The Makhnovists (named for its leader, Nestor Makhno) certainly contained memories of both Marx and Bakunin, as well as touches of the violent Italian and Russian "propagandists of the deed," the classic bombers and assassins, but also the memory of the Paris Commune, which was the "government" that ruled Paris for thirteen months after France's loss in the Franco-Prussian War and included the reopening of workplaces as cooperatives, including a federation of delegates bound by imperative mandates issued by their electors and subject to recall at any moment, Proudhon's ideas, his and Bakunin's. This is—or was—the first modern attempt at "organized" anarchy, or of revolutionary syndicalism, which means self-management of workplaces without the intervention of third parties such as politicians and bureaucrats, and certainly the abolishment of the wage system, hierarchical control, and private ownership of the means of production (as it was called). This would, in theory, abolish severe inequality—and fear. It may be that syndicalism could work only with a small number of people or in a special time—or place—or in economic or political crises. That may be the key to the Makhnovist Movement—which lasted only a few years in the southern Ukraine and was simultaneously military and political, based on a worker and peasant alliance, a "stateless community of workers" who made their own rules and fought their own battles. It originated in the outskirts of Russia, far from the major centers, near the Sea of Azov, isolated not only from the rest of the world but even from other parts of Russia, and was almost unknown outside of its own region. The war (World War I) was still going on, the Treaty of Brest-Litovsk had not yet been signed, so there was pressure to the west from Austria as well as from Russia itself, and the various splinter groups, for it was the middle of the revolution. The Makhnovists did not create a state, nor was it a utopia of visionaries, but a real concrete revolutionary movement, for a very short time an egalitarian stateless community of workers. I'm a lover of facts and statistics, and when I read about the Makhnovist "region," I want to know how many people were actually involved, hundreds, thousands, millions? The Ukraine had never been organized, politically or militarily. It did not have a common cause, but Makhno, according to Arshinov, became the rallying point for *millions* of peasants and workers, in several regions. The name of his village was Gulyai-Polye, and that was its starting point. Makhno was idolized for his ideas, his political acumen, and his military prowess. It was rumored that he never betrayed his trust, but such canards were common in the romantic eras.

What I remember is my uncle George reading a letter in Yiddish by the light coming between the cracks in the large barn of his farm in Mars, Pennsylvania, to his youngest brother, my father, Harry. We must have been sitting on bales of hay. I was probably fifteen, so the year was 1940. It was a letter from Eliezer (Lazer), the oldest brother, twenty years older than my father, who had stayed in Europe and held onto an acre or two of timber, tobacco, and fishponds. I understood the letter—even then—as being mostly about an uncle (my grandfather's brother) or an uncle by marriage—who was active in the years of the revolution in the Ukraine and fought with an army against the Bolsheviks. I think he was a Yunkel too. I understood that he lived later in poverty, I think in Odessa, and had one of his legs cut off. I am certain that he fought with Makhno, and I remembered that letter when I saw the book on the folding table on upper Broadway. George's farm—twenty miles north of Pittsburgh—was eighty acres, and you had to fight the branches when you drove into it from Route 8, the Butler Pike. He had milk cows, goats, apples, and pears, and a lovely house, overrun in the summer with flies where my aunt Annie, suffering from multiple sclerosis, sat—every time I saw her—at the kitchen table beside the window, surrounded by sticky yellow strips containing hundreds of flies. I think I was petting a goat on his bony head and pulling on his horns while my uncle was reading the letter.

I have written elsewhere how Lazer's son was an officer in the Soviet army and was killed in the battle to retrieve Budapest and how he—Lazer—stayed in hiding with a Christian family during most of the war but was murdered by a German soldier one day when he snuck out, maybe to see the sun or smell the hay. As to the question of how a Jew could join a group of guerillas—for that's what they were—in isolated areas where he would have difficulty practicing his religion, let alone faced by the threat of anti-Semitic acts, given it was rural Ukraine with its historic anti-Semitism, there is the testimony in the book of the absolute and specific forbidding of any attacks on Jews *as* Jews. Makhno was an elusive figure in many ways, but whatever he was he was not a *pogromchik*. The Makhnovists were against the formation of a Ukrainian (or any) state, though they recognized and respected existing nationalities, and many in its revolutionary movement were of Greek, Jewish, Armenian, and Caucasian origin. Abuse of Jews and plundering of Jewish agricultural colonies was specifically—and officially—forbidden and punished severely when discovered.

My only connection with the Russian Revolution was an evening I spent with Kerensky, when I was a graduate student at Columbia University, in the company of an old

friend from Pittsburgh, Savel Kliachko, who was studying at the Russian Institute, at Columbia, preparing to
become a spy or a diplomat, who had met Kerensky and
dragged me with him to Kerensky's apartment in the 130s
near Broadway, to drink tea from a samovar and to listen
to him complain about how Lenin and Trotsky (Vladimir
and Leon) had betrayed him when he was the head of the
provisional government in 1917, just before the Bolsheviks
assumed power. Savel was a fellow student in high school,
and his father played cello for the Pittsburgh Symphony
Orchestra under Fritz Reiner. He was heavy and clumsy
and spoke Russian at home. He did two things for me
for which I remain grateful. He got me a job doing con-
versational English with Dr. Shu, the former minister of
finance under Chiang Kai-Shek, maybe 1949. Shu lived in
Great Neck and hated George Marshall for recognizing
Mao and turning away from Chiang Kai-Shek. Our conversation consisted almost exclusively of him cursing and
ridiculing Marshall, but I didn't care because by visiting
him two hours a day, two days a week, Tuesday and Thurs-
day, I made enough to live on and spend my time reading
and writing. I also charged him for books.

The other thing I'm grateful to Savel for is introducing
me to a lovely Canadian woman I spent some time with in

France, just after they turned the lights on in 1950. Maybe I got it backward—I think I did, and the meetings with Dr. Shu were in the early 1950s. I always felt I was a serious part of history for meeting Kerensky. He was a brilliant windbag. Since I spent my life as a teacher my influence was always indirect, except for the times I spent protesting, marching here and there, making a speech or two. I was a cross between a nihilist and an anarchist, so when I did participate, my beliefs secretly informed and governed my actions, except that I did pay my taxes, registered my car, voted, and served in the army. Easier doing than not doing. In my time. I was the head of a teachers' union (AFT) at a community college in New Jersey, outwitted the administration, led a strike, threatened to join the Teamsters, got amazing benefits for my faculty, was head of the state organization, spoke French and Yiddish at negotiation sessions, and had secret understandings with my opponents whom I publicly argued with at the table. I could never have done that for a lifetime. Except for the invisible machinations, it was—mostly—boring. It was like being in business—my apologies. I could—finally—only do one thing that wasn't oppressive: what I'm doing now.

Shoshana and the Elders

In the middle of all this, for one reason or another, I started thinking of the legend, the myth, of Susanna and the Elders and writing—in my own way—some of the Susanna (Shoshana) stories that occupied my memory. Some contemporary painters reconsider the myth directly (Benton) and some (Picasso), indirectly. It is a well-known story but the source—the Book of Daniel—is not so well known. There it is seen not as an erotic tale but as a question of justice and the need to cross-examine witnesses, who, as in this case, may be false witnesses. I am puzzled why such a myth made its way into a book about death. Maybe love, or love-making, is an interruption or an opposite, as Freud suggests. But why *this* form of love? Maybe it came from a reading of Steven's poem "Peter Quince at the Clavier." It is certainly significant that it was—at least in name—the Elders who lusted for Susanna. If anyone needed something to take their minds off of the impending future, it was they. It is fascinating that in all the well-known paintings, those of Tintoretto, Rubens, Rembrandt, and others, the Elders are not bald or even thin-haired; they are robust, muscular men in their sixties and fifties, even in their forties. None is in his seventies or eighties—and, if they are, say, in contemporary renderings they are doubly ironic and destructive of the very idea. I like that Thomas Hart Benton included himself as one of the elders in his version. I guess I am an elder too (I am truly an elder), and the Shoshanas I spy on and am moved by are women from my own past about whom I re-think and fantasize while I am resting or listening to Fats Waller or Bach. They become, in my mind, what they once were, as I become what I was. This is invisible and private; no one is abused. The fact is that no one was ever abused, though we'd have to hear from them, wouldn't we? Wallace Stevens has an odd take on the elders. What they experience—in the poem—is a kind of music, since, as he says, "Music is feeling, then, not sound; / And thus it is that what I feel, / Here in this room, desiring you, / Thinking of your blue-shadowed silk, / Is music." "It is like the strain / Waked in the elders by Susanna" so that "the red-eyed" elders, watching Susanna, "felt / The basses of their beings throb / In witching chords." It is "melody" that went on belittling them: "Susanna's music touched the bawdy strings / Of those white elders." It is a gorgeous poem; and its gorgeosity has carried it since 1915. But what Stevens says is astounding. And, at bottom, it is she—in Stevens's poem—who entices the elders, and no one is innocent.

When I took an overnight ferry from Athens to Crete, in 1976, I found myself, after a few hours keeping company with an Englishwoman named Mavis, and when we landed—in the morning—in Heraklion, it seemed clear that we were going to travel together for the few weeks she would be in Crete. We rented a room together and went swimming naked our first evening. She had been there before, on this very beach, among some reeds in a remote part of the town. She was quite beautiful, except one of her arms—I think the left—was withered and rather useless. It was smashed, she told me, when she fell off a horse and the horse fell full force on her arm, breaking it in several places. I think the operations were botched and she finally gave up. Maybe some critical muscle and bone had been destroyed. She was in her mid- or late forties when we met (I was fifty-one), and I think she had carried that arm for about ten years. She was married but separated, and as it turned out, she lived with her mother-in-law. It was my very first connection with an Englishwoman, and I was struck by how strong and integrated her feelings were and how freely and powerfully she expressed them. I understood a certain kind of matriarchy for the very first time, though I didn't know exactly what her caste and class were. I understood though that by common consent she and her husband's mother were in perfect agreement that he—the son and husband—was a total shit and was exiled for good. In our travels through Crete we sometimes slept in the same bed together and sometimes in separate rooms. We weren't, in the beginning, lovers. She had a friend—in Chania, the other end of the northern coast of Crete—probably twenty years younger than me. She had met him the previous summer (it was May or June then) and was planning to see him again. I remember we drove by (improvised) cab, a Mercedes, on the main highway to Chania and stayed there for the rest of her time before she had to go back to England, eating our meals together, talking, reading, swimming. She left one day late in the morning to meet her friend and came back early in the afternoon and lay on her bed, crying. I don't know exactly what went on but he was, what?—inconsiderate, insensitive, selfish, maybe cruel—certainly not what she had come all the way to Crete for. She had about two or three more days left, and she turned to me with affection and desire—for the first time. We spent hours in bed together, in her room and in mine and were—finally—very close. She left from the town square by bus late one afternoon, and when I put her bags underneath the bus and leaned down to kiss her goodbye she held onto me with a kind of desperation. She was sobbing on the bus when it left the square. We wrote letters to each other for two or three years. Shoshana.

Recently, I found myself sitting on one of my favorite park benches on Riverside Drive and 111th where the wide stone stairs lead down to the Tot Lot, and after that the river walk and the wide river. Next to a metal garbage can with an overloaded black sack in it, a man lay on his back sleeping, four or five of his own black sacks, probably loaded with clothes, beside him, as well as a tiny violin, but nothing I could see to entice passers-by to drop coins into his tattered gray hat, which anyway covered his face against the sun. On the bench beside him was a pair of lovers, kissing, touching, their arms and legs entwined as if they hadn't seen each other in over an hour and might be separated for as long as two or even three in the coming afternoon. Down the road, to my left, was a very old and tiny woman that I had seen there several times and had even tried to talk to on one occasion. She was stone deaf and couldn't hear one word I said. She had told me where she was born (Chicago), how many children she had (three), that two of them were already dead, and that she had lived in the same apartment (across the street) for fifty-five years. Across from me was a couple—I thought they were a couple—she, extremely thin and he, hugely fat. She was reading the Sunday *Times*, carefully folding and refolding the pages; he was on his phone and wandered off several times to have a smoke. They never talked to each other or made any kind of contact, leading me to believe they were merely sitting beside one another, strangers, sharing an iron armrest, the way you do at a movie; only the armrest is wooden there. I saw him later that day, same shirt, same belly, walking up Broadway, smoking a cigarette.

It was a busy spot, dogs with their owners, children with nursemaids or parents, or since it was in the reach of Columbia and Barnard, students lugging books and phoning each other. It was sixty years ago that I was seeing a Barnard student, out of convenience mostly, so I was shocked that year when in February she sent me a birthday letter expressing her love. I don't remember where she was from or what she was studying, but I know I liked her

reticence and her spareness. She had a keenness for poetry and her single favorite line was Chaucer's "and *smalle
fowles machen melodie*" from *The Canterbury Tales,* which
we read to each other. I left for France the following August or September, and by complete accident we met again
in Paris where she and her mother were staying in a hotel
where friends of mine were living. Her mother had to be
in her early or middle forties and was graceful and direct,
with the gift of finding the precise, sometimes shocking,
words to express her ideas or feelings. She was just about
old enough to be my "young mother," so it wasn't a case
of an old man looking at a young girl, nor was she herself
flirtatious. If anything, she was encouraging to her daughter and sort of pushing us together. Only now at my age,
reconsidering, rethinking the connection am I aware how
attractive the mother was to me, and that is the peculiar
nature of this Shoshana with this elder. But I only saw her
two or three times before she returned to America. Before
they both returned. It is out of these particulars that I did
my relooking, my spying. Internal as it was. That I longed
for the mother, forget the thin daughter. Shoshana.

Cemeteries in Lambertville

As far as I can see there are two cemeteries in Lambert-ville, and that is where its inhabitants have been buried, put to rest, as we say, aside from those who have been put to *their* rest by the match or by drowning in the canal and eaten by turtles, or planted in the backyard, or the woods, or left to rot in a garage somewhere, or a toolshed or an empty chicken coop. One of the graveyards is off the main highway to the north of town, and it's called the Holcombe Riverside Cemetery because it's near the river, though not at its side. It's a level and well-kept cemetery, with many small American flags displayed. The other graveyard is at the south end of town, up a very steep hill, such that if you stand at the farthest—southern—end you get a beautiful view of town and countryside. It's called Mt. Hope. The ground is very uneven, full of small hills, and the grass badly needs mowing. I can't tell which cemetery is the older; the dates of the dead seem more or less the same; and I recognize local names in both cemeteries. Maybe Mt. Hope is a little fancier; the crosses are bigger and there is an occasional small stone house for the dead one to live in. There seem to be Protestants and Catholics more or less scattered everywhere, in both places, maybe some atheists. I didn't see any Jewish names or six-pointed stars, though a local funeral director says there is a small corner—in Mt. Hope—where Jews are gathered together. Ethnic and religious groups seem to stay close to each other in two places in particular, cemeteries and summer resorts. The Jersey Shore, with its Irish, Jewish, Methodist enclaves, is an example. Me, if I'm buried in this town, it will probably be near some Jews I don't know or just dumped in with the goyim, as I am now on the upper side, more or less good neighbors all, and welcoming to Jews who are more or less hornless—as they are beardless—walking up and down Main or Union or Bridge.

I phoned Harold Schechter today—after rereading sections of his book *The Whole Death Catalog*, to hear his views on a few things I was unsure of. He has the dearest take on things, he spares nothing—and no one—yet he's funny, believable, honest—and sane. I asked him about the proverbial worm, as in "worms will try / that long preserved virginity" and he talked about "worms" as a conventional and symbolic term, not really the culprit if the coffin were tight and water had not softened the wood, worms really referring to earlier days when bodies were dumped without protection into the ground, or just with a flimsy covering, maybe wood, or even reeds. Maggots would be at play then too, fly babies, as well as vermin of various sorts, and even birds when the body was sufficiently exposed. But the English poets should have realized that—virgin or not—the dead body itself undoes the tenuous but desperate hold on life by its own natural devices, the corpse life. It occurs in stages: with your heart no longer pumping, the blood sinks to the lowest parts of your body, your back and buttocks (if you are lying face up). Those areas will become purple-red while your face and chest turn white, what Harold calls "ghastly white." Your muscles start to stiffen, your temperature drops, and you become stiff. A stiff. Rigor mortis sets in. You remain that way for one to three days, then the muscles grow flaccid again. In the next stage, bloat, the bacteria in the intestinal tract generate (or continue to generate) gas, but since our colon and sphincter have stopped functioning we can't discharge the gas. The body becomes corpulent, the pressure of the gas causes the eyes to bulge, pushes the intestines out through the rectum and forces foul bloody fluid through the mouth, nose, and other orifices. The skin changes color, from green to purple and finally—to black. Bloat lasts about a week, and the next stage is putrefaction and decay. The body "liquefies," giant putrid blisters appear on the skin; the hair, nails, and teeth loosen, the brain "oozes through the ears or bubbles from the mouth," the belly bursts and "the internal organs dissolve in an unspeakable soup," and the stench is overpowering. Then the corpse—finally—turns into "dry remains." Harold is so good here—as he is elsewhere—that I have borrowed, i.e., stolen outright from him. But I'm giving him the credit, which should free me of standing trial for plagiarism, the specialty, horror, and righteous disavow of my former colleagues at various towers here and there, given to excessive talk and much indignation. Harold told me, when I asked him about his own planned mode, that he wanted to go out to sea on a carved log, much like a Viking, reciting a favorite Edda—maybe remembering a joke (in his last sleep) while the flames consumed him. I hope he gets his wish.

If you don't want the poor body to suffer such indignities, the issue of cremation as an alternative comes up. Cremation is (officially) opposed by the three Western religions but is embraced by "right-thinking" secularists and escapees, my closest friends. I wrote a poem about it, in 1975, called "Rotten Angel." I ask the state's permission to bury my body on the small wooded island on the Delaware River a half-mile or so south of my former house there, and I have an extended image of the Malachamavet swimming across the seventy-five or so feet of water to the Pennsylvania shore through the algae, gnats, and mosquitoes, holding his breath and closing his eyes as I used to do, going back and forth during the long summers, generally in the early evening, once rather late returning in the dark to my house, my bathing suit flung over my shoulder, I remember saying in that poem that I didn't want to be dumped into a small pine or mahogany box and put on the mantle. I wanted to hang onto what we call "life" as long as possible.

If cremation is forbidden by Orthodox Jews and Muslims and is optional for most Christians, it is standard practice among Hindus and Buddhists, though earth burial is permitted by Buddhists, at least Western ones. Cremation was coupled by many odd customs in each of the cultures that practiced it, as was also earth burial and simple abandonment in this or that either sacred or foolhardy space. Since the Greeks and Romans practiced burning it was looked upon as "pagan" by the first Chris-

tians and was finally outlawed—criminalized—by Charlemagne in 789 CE, and for the next thousand years, even
more, earth burial was the only method practiced in the
West. It was only in the late nineteenth century that cremation began to be practiced on a wide scale, when earth
burial was criticized by a group of medical experts as a
threat to public health. Five pounds of ashes, including a
few bones, could be held in glass, wooden, or cardboard
boxes. I have gone to four or five cremation ceremonies
and wrote a poem ("Bob Summers' Body") about one of
them. Many religious leaders, including Jewish, argue that
the eventual resurrection of the body requires an intact
corpse. But I doubt if any God would prefer one form of
dry remains to another. By 1941 there were two hundred
crematoria in the United States, triple that, or quadruple,
now. Though a certain amount of excessive ceremony and
ridiculous consumerism have taken over the burn houses,
the belief that incineration is more sanitary and more aesthetic still underlies the practice.

Myself, I am still stuck, but my ambivalence may be
only a method of—hopefully—delaying the onset. My
father was embalmed and my mother was talked into a
mahogany casket (for him) and a police (motorcycle) es-
cort to the graveyard. This *after* Nancy Mitford's book on

the stupidities and excesses of American funerals and the stranglehold of the funeral industry. I talked my mother into a plain pine coffin and a favorite summer dress, and made sure that the coffin was screwed tight. She died in Miami Beach and was buried alongside my father in the cemetery at Opa-locka. I myself officiated at her funeral that my son and daughter, in their early thirties, a handful of Florida relatives, a few old friends and neighbors, and a couple of professional weepers attended. I talked for twenty or twenty-five minutes about her life in America and some of the joys—and sorrows—she experienced. I think I sang a few bars from her favorite song, "Melancholy Baby," and told a few (gentle) Jewish jokes. She would have been pleased. Afterward we had some refreshments at her apartment on West Avenue, facing the bay. I was helped in the preparation by two poets who were living then in Florida, Susan Mitchell and Laura Mullen. I did hire a rabbi—for a hundred bucks—to say a few prayers in Hebrew, for she would have liked that. He was surprised—and offended—that I didn't want him to "officiate" and kept asking me questions about her life as if he were preparing a eulogy, though I kept telling him "no" as if I were correcting a stubborn child. And I had my way.

In the 1980s I did visit my father's site in order to

gather material for my long poem "Bread Without Sugar." I remember my mother and I were driven to the cemetery in Opa-locka, by a ninety-five-year-old madman who had cans of gefilte fish on the backseat, probably for seven dollars less than a cab would have cost, and we had trouble finding the grave since the records were in the hands of a new owner; and trash was thrown over the fence near the grave by the disrespectful residents of that town—but all that is described in my poem. My father, born on a farm in southern Ukraine, died in the American tropics; my mother, born in Bialystok, was buried in a swamp. I had no opportunity, or couldn't find the language, or couldn't represent the "facts" accurately to my father, who never understood my life as a writer and probably imagined it was the life of a devoted and poor scholar, as he understood it, and this was the source of much of my grief for him—probably his for me. My mother lived to see my "success," and though I have many of her bad habits, my life with her was unbearably difficult. She "expired" while I was on a plane, much delayed, from St. Louis or Chicago, on the way from Iowa City to Miami. It was a relief, I have to say, to start living without her, though I was already in my sixties. To wake up at the Forté Towers, at 1100 West Avenue, Miami Beach, Florida, fully alone, was joyous.

The grief I had was for the life she led—or didn't—though I know that it is presumptuous to say it. To describe our family as dysfunctional is an understatement. All during the long autumn of their lives, my father and mother argued endlessly, in Yiddish and English, slamming doors, walking in and out of rooms. They had a short respite—in their winter—but my father only lasted four years and died in 1969, probably seventy-two years old, but he didn't know exactly.

The good memories were of Saturday night, my father at work, and Libby, my grandmother, Thelma, our maid, Ida, and myself eating the ridiculous spaghetti—they called it that—that we ate every Saturday for supper. I was under ten. The second (good) memory was eight, nine years later, eating a late breakfast, my mother and I discussing the books I was reading then, a few of which she read, though she had more or less given up reading since—she said—she was blind in one eye. *Studs Lonigan, The Magic Mountain, Babbit, Look Homeward Angel, U.S.A.*—these were some of the novels. She liked to identify with Thomas Wolfe's Eliza Gant, Eugene's mother, though she was nothing like her. Two other memories of the time before my tenth birthday, the first riding into town (of a Saturday) in a speeding, rocking, clanging, or-

ange-colored streetcar, going to a movie (and stage show)
downtown, and eating apple pie and chocolate ice cream
at Isaly's before we walked over to the store my father
managed on Liberty Avenue, the Palace Credit Clothing
Company, where I entertained the salesmen by drawing
likenesses in a notebook I carried with me; and the second, on the edge, so to speak: my mother and a girlhood
friend of hers taking a shower together in the basement
of our house (they were both maybe thirty-three; I was
nine). Her friend's son and I running through the house,
maybe playing marbles outside, maybe looking at baseball
cards. His name was Morty. I was shocked at seeing them
naked; I guess Morty was too. But, for a few minutes, the
two women were enjoying a freedom that was rare in their
lives. We had one bathroom in the house, but it didn't have
a shower. Potatoes and apples were in the fruit cellar, coal
in the coal cellar (two little rooms), and the icebox was
at the bottom of the stairs leading up to the kitchen. My
mother's friend (Bessie) went to the Jewish Home for the
Aged quite early, maybe when she was sixty. I remember
on a visit her telling my mother she still had her marbles,
so "fuck off with your pity." My father and I mostly spent
Sundays together on the Avenue, Upper 5th, on the Hill,
where the wholesale houses were located, eating amazing

roast beef sandwiches at Goldstein's, and afterward driving to look at model homes in the newer suburbs.

I don't know where the Muslim view of cremation comes from, but the Jewish tradition looks on burning as a direct contradiction of custom and law. The Talmud of course is long and leaves nothing unturned, but I can't find *specific* references to cremation in the Bible itself. One shocked writer says it is forbidden in any and every circumstance to reduce the dead to ash in a crematorium. He calls it an offensive act that "does violence to the spirit and letter of Jewish law" and refers to the practice as *pagan*. Tacitus, the Roman historian, I learned from this writer, remarked on the Jewish *abhorrence* of cremation as a distinguishing characteristic of the Jews—that they buried rather than burned their dead. This same writer related that a famous rabbi ruled that in special circumstances ashes could be buried, but at a minimum of eight feet from the nearest grave and that neither Shiva could be observed nor Kaddish recited for such. By providing that they be incinerated they had given up all their right to posthumous privileges and practices. Yet many Jews, including those who would call themselves good Jews, whatever that means, have chosen to be cremated. The writer I am referring to,

Maurice Lamm, may be speaking for the Orthodox. The last five Jews I have spoken to who are into their years, when I asked them, they all said they weren't sure. Three were poets, one a teacher of business at a community college, and one a famous Greek—and Spanish—translator.

If everything is provided for, in Lamm's book, from the placing of the coffin at the very bottom of the grave to the burial of amputated limbs, from the Burial Kaddish with its affirmation that the deceased will be raised up to everlasting life, to marital relations of survivors, from the ritual of reinterment to the respect for a gravestone, it is not only for the upholding of the ancient customs but for respect for the dead one and honoring his or her life. Tough rules are often, if not always, difficult to live with. Lamm says that mirrors are covered because there should be no vanity or because since man was made in the image of God, then the image of God, which might have diminished (in beauty?) should not be made visible. Harold says that mirrors are covered so the malevolent or demonic spirit of the dead cannot pass through since mirrors, à la Dracula, have the power to steal or house human souls. Just as the wearing of dark (black) clothes hides the living from the malevolent spirit though I'm sure that Harold doesn't believe this. Lamm says we shouldn't wear shoes during Shiva but go in stocking feet or slippers because—again—of a disregard of vanity and for personal mortification. Harold wears tight-fitting shoes for his mortification, even to bed. Lamm writes a great deal on the afterlife, the soul's eternal existence, immortality, resurrection of the dead. Harold describes the beliefs of many cultures on the subject but doesn't reveal his own. I suspect that, since he will have a Viking death, he will have a Viking afterlife, in Valhalla, complete with reindeer meat and liquor and sleep under a stinking bear's skin by a giant fireplace, burning whole hemlock trees, and during the night breaking glass windows with the sound of his snoring. And it will take him the entire night to digest the goose he has eaten and the side of cow and the buttocks of a pig and the goat stew and the fruit pie. He has heard that someone from the Southland has landed three small boats on the great unnamed continent his people have already conquered and for this reason he has determined to return, this time to stay.

Haymarket Square

In 1948, when I was twenty-three, the former vice president under FDR, from 1936 to 1944, ran against Truman on the Progressive ticket for the U.S. presidency. He had been, first, the secretary of agriculture, under Roosevelt, and then the secretary of commerce from 1932 to 1940. In 1944 Roosevelt was too sick—and too busy with the war and postwar considerations—and he left the choice of vice president up to the party hacks, who chose Harry Truman instead of Henry A. Wallace. Roosevelt's words were "clear it with Sidney," Sidney Hillman, head of the Amalgamated Clothing Workers of America, who decided who the future president would be. Wallace, who anticipated and opposed the Cold War, was too radical for the Democrats. It was a time of strong anti-Communist (really anti-left) rhetoric and the beginning of McCarthyism. The sentiment had already crept down even to the Pittsburgh police, and I was accused (because I was on the

streets at one a.m. and admitted to having been at a meeting of the local Progressive Party) of being a Communist.
The left, by the beginning of the twentieth century, con-
sisting of labor unions, the nascent Socialist party, and
the IWW, was seen as the enemy by the right-wing corporations, the newspapers, college presidents, Southern
spokesmen, and most priests and ministers; but before
Socialists and Communists came the Anarchists who, by
the 1880s, were the principal bugaboos and hobgoblins.
There was a congress of the Anarchist Party in Pittsburgh
in 1883, and their platform called for an eight-hour day,
the end of child labor, equal pay for whites and blacks and
for men and women, the right to organize unions and to
bargain collectively, safety regulations and unemploy-
ment insurance. No mention of bombs but certainly, at
the time, quite radical.

In Chicago, in the fall of 1885, twenty-two unions
combined into one large organization and adopted a fiery
resolution opposing anti-labor tactics on the part of governments and corporations, and the following spring, on
May 3, 1886, in front of the McCormick Harvester Works
(in Chicago) where strikers were fighting scabs, the police fired into a crowd, wounding many and killing four.
A rally was called for the next day in Haymarket Square,

and 3,000 people assembled. "As storm clouds gathered, the crowd dwindled to a few hundred," says Howard Zinn in his *People's History of the United States*, and "a detachment of 180 policemen showed up and ordered the (small) crowd to disperse. A bomb then exploded in the midst of the police wounding 60, of whom 7 later died. The police fired into the crowd, killing several people, and wounding 200."

There was no evidence that the anarchists were responsible for the bomb; indeed, it could have been an agent provocateur, but eight anarchists were arrested for inciting murder even though only one was present at the Haymarket, and he was speaking when the bomb exploded. They were all found guilty and sentenced to death, and a year after the trial a printer, an upholsterer, and an organizer were hung and a carpenter committed suicide in his cell. It became a cause célèbre, and there were protests in England, France, Holland, Russia, Italy, and Spain. The new governor of Illinois, John Altgeld, denounced what had happened and pardoned the remaining prisoners. It was a political awakening for thousands, as the Sacco-Vanzetti case would later be.

All across the industrial cities of the United States, the first week of May, there was a state of quasi-hysterical euphoria. Various labor organizations, beginning as early as 1884, had set May 1, 1886, as the date when the eight-hour workday would become standard, and labor unions were preparing for a general strike in support of the idea. This was the true beginning of May Day, which started in Chicago and spread throughout the whole world. When I was a boy, May first was something else. It was the day you hired a truck and moved to another apartment. Moving Day. Period. *Our* Labor Day is celebrated the first Monday in September, though it's more the day you dock your boat and go back to the city; or it's the day you stop wearing white shoes and white ducks—at least it used to be—or it's the day before you go back to school, though if you're at college, teacher *or* student, you may have gone back a week or two earlier so as to be tortured by the heat. The reason it was celebrated in September rather than on May first was—and is—to disconnect it from the International Workers' Day because of the heavy presence of Communists and Anarchists. May Day. Labor Day is also an important sales day, second only to Black Friday.

The Haymarket Riot was always important—almost holy—to me; I even imagined—fantasized—that I was present there as a young man listening to the speeches in English and German. That would have made me a young poet in 1885 or 1890, which I am sure would not have been any easier than being a young poet in 1946, after the war, especially if you came from the provinces—as I did. I was lucky though, since I was only seven dollars away from New York and had the G.I. Bill to fall back on. I have written about this somewhere else. I have also written that I'm attracted to the prophets. Amos, Ezekiel, Isaiah, Hosea, among others. That although they were interested in justice, as I am, and even kindness, their purposes were the worship of God; they believed that one strayed from justice when he or she was not godly. And whatever I mean by justice, I think it has little to do with the existence of God or his worship. Thus my alliance with the prophets is only a kind of temporary friendship. We leave each other when they put on the phylacteries and start waving their index fingers. Yet, when I reduce their vision to its poetry, I am at home. All artists get away from their own religious upbringing in order to arrive at a condition of faith or love. That's putting on the gloves—or taking them off—but it's a position that sustained me then—and now. Though all of this has taken on a certain distance, a dislocation, even a vagueness, that probably has more to do with age than with anything else.

Certainly I was never hung or electrocuted, for here I

sit drinking Eight O'Clock in the hot sun just after listening to the Ink Spots and their version of "My Prayer" and "If I Didn't Care." I love "Waiter, waiter, percolator," and I am close enough to Presbyterian bells and train whistles, which generate memory much more than pills or psychoanalysis ever did. I can even tell how fast a train is going from the degree of frenzy in the whistles, I can almost tell how long it is, though I can't for the life of me tell what it's carrying. Polluted oil, I think.

Lost in Time

It was yesterday, September 24, 2013, while driving north along the Pennsylvania side of the Delaware River that I had my wild argument with time. That was one of the most perfect rides I took—every day—all during the 1970s, crossing the bridge from Riegelsville, New Jersey, to Riegelsville, Pennsylvania, and driving up 611 to my home on old 611, between the canal and the river, back from my work—teaching, negotiating, going to meetings, and writing in my small windowless office at what was then Somerset County College and today is Raritan. For I was, after I passed Riegelsville, Pennsylvania, only repeating, retracing, my steps, driving north as I always did, day after day; and this drive was simultaneously occurring as part of a continuum of the earlier time; forgiving and forgetting the passage of thirty-some years that had intervened. It was not that I was "lost in time" or "forgetful," or suffering from either illusion or delusion. Although I was suffering from what I have to call temporal identity, though it was a pleasant kind of suffering and not a crisis of any sort.

It was an issue of "time," there was no question. So, scholar that I am, I managed to retrieve whatever I could on the issue through the books I had available on my second floor, including work by—or on—Immanuel Kant and Parmenides, Aristotle and Spinoza, Augustine and Hegel, as well as my three huge dictionaries of philosophy, and on the advice of Lynne Sharon Schwartz I reread *The Magic Mountain*, chapter after chapter, but I must say that Bergson was the one I remembered the most and who bespoke my own experience the keenest. At least on this subject; or—to put it simply—his was the name that popped up, not Marx or Augustine, when I was suddenly seized, and his concept of past and present and the present use of the past were most useful to me in trying to realize my state, driving north on Highway 611 by the Delaware River. If I was lost in time it was not metaphorically but most literally and physically and intellectually. Maybe it wasn't a matter of being "lost" but redirected, as one thing became another, as they became each other. I adored the view to my right halfway up to my old highway, the hills and woods across the water in New Jersey, the eddies and perturbations in the river itself, which I knew so well from floating down and swimming there and, in the hottest months, just walking across the rocks where the water only came up to my knees. When I reached the island where the Malachamavet visited, I stared through the locusts and sycamores to where I knew the path was, and if it was very late spring and summer when the little peninsula out there became a true island I would stare lovingly at the smooth river stones and remember how many times I flung them, shotlike, always doing the classical maneuvers preparatory to the throw, half-bending with my hands at my knees to see the results. I looked out and over to see if I had once again broken the record. And raised my left hand in a shout, though I was all alone. Most of all, it was the half-mile walk to the lock—and back—every night before I went to sleep. And standing by a cement wall with the water rushing down, sometimes for thirty or forty minutes. Feeling the sadness in that water, for it was literal time rushing by, irretrievable time. I may have been fifty then, and my spirits may have lifted a little as I walked past a ruin that I was thinking of restoring and as I approached my house with its porch light on and a duller light in the back, which was surely from a low-watt lightbulb in the kitchen.

I don't know if the afterlife, as we imagine it, is a place

of peace, serenity, and quiet or a place of joy and unbe-
lievable energy, but whatever it might be it would have to
compete with that little place in Raubsville, that acre on
the river and the life I had there. There is a photograph of
the house itself as it faces old 611 the week, maybe the very
day, we bought it. The "mud" covering the stones is dirty
and needs painting, the large bushes are not yet planted,
and it's long before the state all but ruined the houses on
that road by forcing the owners to put their buildings up
on stilts, with wooden steps going up (and down). Our
house belonged in the mud and it was—then—separated
from the ground underneath it by one maybe six-inch
stone step. It was up that step and into the living room
that I and a friend of mine dragged and pushed a very
heavy upright piano I had bought at an auction for seven
dollars and started my daughter on her musical education. Such was my life then. We ended up with a large
comfortable home, a rich garden of strawberries, toma-
toes, eggplant, string beans, lettuce, and such, and I must
say that I always knew how special the house was even
from the moment I first bought it—in 1968—for seven
thousand dollars, again at an auction. There was a very
long wraparound porch, on the south and the east side,
there were swallow apartment houses under the eaves—at

the south—there was a great black birch tree in the side yard and—across old 611—there was another building that once was a garage which I rebuilt and turned into a large studio, overlooking the river. There is no question that it was paradisiacal, a foretaste as it were. We used to float down the six or so miles from Easton on large inner tubes and land on our property for beer and sandwiches. Down the road—a hundred yards away—was the old hotel, a bar on the first floor and small rooms on the second where the barge men stopped to eat and rest and—I hear—have their *petites alliances* in the small bedrooms. Routes 611 and 32 south (to Bristol, Pennsylvania), there was such a hotel every six or seven miles, many of them still standing, some of them good restaurants, but none of them whorehouses. We always had a large New Year's Eve party with dozens of guests, and in the early summer my son, David, had his annual party, his friends who went to work after high school and married young, drinking beer from the half-keg, and my daughter and a few of her musician friends standing together, a little lost in the company, probably uncomfortable with the music.

The religions argue endlessly about the heavenly place, and anti-Semitic economists—whose principal vision, that of creating perfection, derives specifically from the mad Jews, from *we* mad Jews—stick ice picks into each other, but they all tend to agree that it will be an extension or a version of our lives here on this sweet planet. We may be burdened with wings or virgins or bows and arrows or books or even a delicious horse, but it's earthly. For me, it's the memory of a few good places, a house, a hotel in the Pennsylvania mountains, a room overlooking the square in Oaxaca, the art room on the seventh floor in the old libraries of the Cathedral of Learning in Pittsburgh. It wasn't supposed to last forever. These afterlives tend to be places of justice, or of beauty, or of what could be called serenity, freedom from physical and mental pain, of confusion and anxiety and even boredom; and places of "active joy," lovemaking, swimming. There will be good food and no indigestion. In that movie of my youth, *The Green Pastures*, you even meet and talk to someone called "God," an old African American with a white cottony beard. There was a version of him on the cover of the magazine called *The Sun*. I studied it for hours. It was astounding to learn that we weren't made in God's image, as it says in Genesis, but he was made from ours. In the movie he spoke English, not Hebrew, Babylonian, or Egyptian. Moses and his mother, Miriam, would have gotten a kick out of it.

My Sister Sylvia

I have written more than a few poems about my sister, one year and one month older than me, dead at nine from spinal meningitis, which, as I remember, cloaked itself as a common cold, a very brief stay in the hospital, followed by a small white coffin in our living room, dozens of aunts, uncles, cousins, my father and mother in agony and at wit's end, my mother's breakdown a few days later, a local doctor, Dr. Dunn, nursing her back to the living, and a long lifetime of depression on her part and sadness and bewilderment on the part of my father and myself.

Any token, any memory, of Sylvia was destroyed, no photos, no books, toys, clothes, not even a favorite pillow or doll. By unspoken agreement we weren't allowed to mention her, or say her name, or celebrate her birthday, or in any way acknowledge that she even existed. It wasn't until my mother was in her late eighties that I deliberately mentioned my sister by name—Sylvia—and that I began to talk about her and that my mother—in great relief by that time—almost welcomed it.

For my part, I have for years wondered how it would have been if she hadn't died, what it would have been like having a sister in my teenage years, and later. What my life would have been like, how our family would have fared, and—most of all—what she herself would have been like growing up, and as an adult. I have long since abandoned *la petite guerre* I had for so many years with Ida and *l'autre guerre* with Harry. Forty, fifty years ago. I have followed the adage, "Forgive but don't forget." I think I felt at one time that I wasted years taking care of them instead of myself. Though I know they would have seen it differently and I also know I *was* taking care of myself and I was making the choices that, at the time, at the *times*, seemed possible for me. Nothing was lost, even if there was sadness. But if Sylvia had survived, the load would have been partly—perhaps mostly—hers and not exclusively mine. I say it in pure selfishness.

Sylvia was a wild and beautiful girl. I was probably a bit of a problem for her since I was the male heir and I was unbearably innocent and skipped a grade so that for two years we were in the same class in school. I think she loved me dearly, but she was always the leader, especially when it came to mischief, which seemed to compromise the love. I really don't remember a whole lot. I think we slept in the same room since our house had three bedrooms, one for my mother and father, one for Thelma the maid, and ours, the third. When my grandmother, Libby, came to live with us, I don't remember where we slept. That would have been for two or three years in the early 1930s, before she remarried. We lived in a rather small house, and we were close to each other physically as well as emotionally, and I have a vivid memory, but for the life of me I only remember three things clearly—the rest is shadowy and evanescent. I remember we had two peach trees and one was identified as Sylvia's and one as mine, or one *was* Sylvia and one *me;* and I remember the two of us being half-lost in the woods across the street from our house and some older boys forcing us to take off our clothes, or enough to bare our genitals; and I remember walking into the living room where Sylvia was being upbraided for some offense or other and being ordered to my room. She was lying on the floor with her legs akimbo and one arm under her head, stubborn and disrespectful, and my parents were each sitting on upholstered chairs looking angrily down at her. I knew at once it was something sexual and a severe violation—at least from my parents' point of view. Though I knew nothing then of the sexual, I knew it instinctively. When I think of it now I am certain she was caught "touching herself" (a kinder word than the other), and I think, with horror, of what was said to her, the lies, the teachings, the elucidation of the forbidden. How banal—and dishonest—it seems to me now. How refined and knowledgeable she must have been, already, to see it. I see it now in the same light. I always thought I understood the simplicity of my mother's and father's beliefs, but I was as often as not surprised.

I called my daughter today to hear again her version of the huge argument she had with her grandmother when she was fifteen and visiting her in Florida. I thought it might give me a clue somehow to Ida's attitude and behavior toward her daughter, Sylvia. But, of course, it was a *version*, and my mother also had a version, I'm sure. According to Rachael, my daughter, she was in Miami for a week, in April—probably 1974—I think. She met a girl her own age, from some northern city, Boston, Detroit, Chicago, who was likewise visiting *her* grandmother, and they spent a lot of time together, at the pool, in the lobby, at each of the grandmothers' apartments, as it turned out, on the same floor of the building. Ida, according to Rachael, resented the time she spent with her new friend, and wanted Rachael to stay in her apartment and not be away from her. There were no boys or late nights involved. The girls wanted to go down to the pool, but Ida wanted them to wait until she was ready. It ended up with Ida throwing Rachael out and telling her to leave and not come back. This to a fifteen-year-old with no resources. I am only going into this to try to guess what the relationships would have been with Sylvia if she had survived to fifteen or sixteen or, for that matter, into her adult years. A boy, a man-child, in that Jewish American immigrant bourgeois culture, was given immense freedom, really little supervision. Although it might have been exaggerated, that lack of supervision—even interest—on the part of my family. Maybe even neglect. The girl was relatively confined, even locked up. My particular family may have represented a distortion or exaggeration even of this practice. Out of their ignorance. My mother, Ida, may have been altogether the wrong mother for a daughter. I remember enough of that world to know how free many young women actually were, free to travel, to sleep over at a friend's house, to pursue an interest. I think Sylvia would have been doomed, that given her spirit she would have been very angry—as she already was—and rebellious. It couldn't have been otherwise.

I wish I had more to remember. My mind goes back to many things that happened to *me*, long before Sylvia's death; but, in spite of the fact that she was so important to me, I have very little to think about as far as she's concerned, and I only realize this now, quite late in my life, as I write about her. Of what I do know, drawn from strong feeling rather than a memory of particulars, is a sense of the utter impossibility of Sylvia being "contained" in the life that was being meted out to her; certainly something conventional and traditional but of an extreme nature in its conventionality and traditionalism, which I'm sure she would not have been capable of bearing. She was born in 1924—in January—so she would have reached her maturity sometime during the Second World War, in 1942 or '43. She might have suddenly left home; or tried to join the service; or married a stranger and gone off with him; or found a new life in some college or other. It was too early in America's evolution to find a comfortable or a peaceful place to be, given her nature. I don't know if political, or sexual, radicalism might have seized her later. It was both too early and, at the same time, too late for feminism. Maybe something connected with the war might have saved her. But, try as I do, I can't find a place for her. From what I know—what I feel—I can't see her in a conventional marriage, a wedding dress, a ceremony in our—Conservative—synagogue, followed by a little house and children; and, if it did somehow happen, it couldn't have lasted long even if divorce wasn't so strongly condemned in our absurd and rigid world. Though things change, and there's scant to fall back on.

I mostly just mourn Sylvia's death, but I'm aware—intensely aware—that what I became, a caretaker, a provider, an overwhelmingly hard worker, was, in some respects, connected to my assuming a new burden because of her death. I would have been so much freer if she lived and I would have known so much more. I realize now, above all else, that I wouldn't have had to spend a long lifetime hunting women down just to understand them. That I might have had a chance to be freer and more comfortable, more *knowledgeable,* if Sylvia only had survived. That I didn't have to domesticate myself. That I could have run off to Brazil.

As far as memory, and remembering very little of the particulars, I must say that I remember details from my own life in a never-ending stream, some when I was two, two and a half years old, matching my remembrance of things with objective fact, as I later did. I feel queasy, I have to say, about the biographical matter, the personalism of it, how it seldom serves a more general use. I am reading a book-length interview of Norman Manea, the Romanian novelist and author of *The Hooligan's Return*, where he indeed writes about himself but always in terms of the death camps, the horrors of Romania, his family, friendships, travel, escape. Never to *display* himself, like some huge exotic bird, at least not that alone. I have tried through my own writing not to give in to this display, but here I am writing a short book about myself and in this section, in this part, I have given myself up maybe for the tenth time, to writing about a woman—I now see her as a woman and not as a girl—who had come a long time ago to stand for womankind for me.

I have several versions of Sylvia as an adult. One of them has her married to a cellist or a violist, I think in Chicago, a gentle, loving man. She has three children, one in his mid-thirties from an early somewhat crazy union and two, much younger, nineteen and twenty-one, with the musician. She has just turned fifty-eight. She went to the conservatory at Oberlin early on to study flute, and much later she got a master's of social work degree at Hunter College in east Harlem. They are involved with musicians, poets, and painters, mostly by the lake, and plan on moving in a few months to Philadelphia, where they both have new jobs. There's been a lot of trouble with the son, drugs and the like, but he seems to have settled down. He is getting an MBA at Pitt. The two younger are both girls. She, Sylvia, is very beautiful, but her face and body bear the burden of a tough life, especially early on. She says she is getting ready for her old age, but her family and her friends just laugh at her. She seems to have some connection with relatives, second and third cousins, in the Midwest and in New York. She goes a few times a year to a nearby Reconstructionist synagogue and is a close friend with the (woman) rabbi, but she's not very active. I always see her at Thanksgiving and one or even two times more during the year. I am living on the West Coast, alone, writing poetry, studying philosophy, practicing my Yiddish and learning Spanish.

The second version has her leaving home at sixteen and going first to New York and then to San Francisco. She is angry, out of touch, and hardly responds to anyone, even to me, though we were close. She had two children with a borderline criminal and con artist before her twentieth birthday, in 1943 when medieval rules prevailed. She is painting, against all odds, and living in poverty. This after giving up her writing. She moved from Farrell, Dos Passos, and Steinbeck to Dawn Powell and Willa Cather, and some of her stories are excellent, but she lost faith in them. I am still in high school at the time and though I am a little in shock I am anxious to visit her on the West Coast. My mother and father are, as usual, silent about it. It's as if *they* ostracized *her*, but they themselves are desperate, proud, and defensive. We hardly talk about it. Her severe bout of sickness, when she was nine, has left her with some brain damage, involving a mild type of expressive aphasia, but she has abandoned her medications. I saw my little nieces once when Sylvia secretly returned to Pittsburgh.

It is possible that my rebellion, starting at maybe eleven or twelve, only replaced Sylvia's. I might have otherwise ended up a pedagogue or a Common Pleas judge. Though it's doubtful since I had my own rage and my own dream. I'd like to make her happy and at peace in one version. Maybe I did.

The Jews at Mt. Hope Cemetery

I was talking to someone on the phone today and I said "die" instead of "bye," which is easy to do if it's six o'clock p.m. and you still have indigestion from the cheesy pound cake you ate at lunch and you've just done the exercises at your boring gym and you're exhausted from the repetitions and your mind is on graveyards. For which I drove down Union, turned left on Bridge between the two gas stations, right on Main, left on Swan, and right up Franklin to Hope Cemetery hard by the street where, to my left, was a small area of plots for sale by Kehilat Hanahar, the Little Schul by the River, one or two I was—I am—considering buying for my own interment. And Anne Marie's—if she chooses, at such an early age, even to consider it. Rabbi Sandy's stone is already planted there, she dead so young, and on top of the stone six or seven pebbles, or petite stones, that presumably visitors had put there as signs of their visitations, as additional memorials, or, as Harold the mythologist said, to keep the dead one from rising from her grave, to weigh her down, at least symbolically. Sandy was well loved and deeply educated in Jewish lore. In addition, when I knew her, before sickness had taken over, she was lighthearted, serious, and easy to talk to, whether the conversation was about things ordinary or—on occasion—extraordinary. I didn't know her at the end when she allied herself with a woman doctor in Lambertville or when she was fighting her disease. It was her replacement, Rabbi Diana, educated at the same Reconstructionist rabbinical college outside Philadelphia, who showed me where Sandy was buried and where the other plots were, on a gigantic hill where I, who grew up in the steep hills of western Pennsylvania, might be more comfortable than on a flat piece of land, if you could imagine inert and lifeless dust experiencing such a weird thing in this life—or, for that matter, in any life—as comfort.

I was beginning to reunite with others, at least as far as graveyards were concerned; and as it happened, there was a small study group the rabbi led—and I joined—that met weekly for a Midrash of sorts, this year on King David as he appeared in First and Second Samuel and in First Kings. We used Robert Alter's translation, with its multitude of scholarly footnotes. It is a magnificent translation, except for the poetry, which is wooden and unmusical—at least to my ears. We are doing it page by page, passage by passage, though it's going more quickly than you might imagine. Given my subject, I turned first to David's old age and death, his sleeping and sleeping *only* with Abishag, supposedly for comfort—and warmth—the ferocious scolding by the court prophet Nathan, and the admonitions, on David's deathbed, to his chosen replacement, Solomon, to not forget the "disloyalty" of his enemies, including Joab, who was his comrade for fifty years, and to take appropriate action. The real beginning of his fall from grace began with his seduction of Bathsheba and the planned murder of her loyal and gullible husband, Uriah, involving the sinister cooperation of the field commander Moab and the unnecessary deaths of other troops by the walls of the Ammonites' royal city, Rabbah. It was a warrior society, and my impulse is to compare it with other warrior cultures, say the Achaeans who conquered Troy. The major difference is that David's nation was driven by the belief that their God was immediately in control of the battles they fought and—moreover—allotted victory or defeat based on the consistency—even the intensity—of that belief and the ethics that underlay it, and on obedience to that ethics. It is true that every tribal culture had its God and sacrifice was made to him (or her), and the warrior's behavior had to have a certain consistency and an "ethics," but the Israeli God was perhaps more stubborn, exclusive, and single-minded than the other, say, Canaanite Gods. The Achaean Gods entered the battle of Troy and *intervened* for their favorites, true, but there was a variety of opinions among them and therefore a kind of ensuing confusion. It is the obsessive religious belief of David that directs *his* behavior and that of his subjects. He is violent, cruel, murderous, short-tempered, and unforgiving, like any Greek or Trojan hero, but different in his single-hearted passion. Homer's epics may describe a period of time as much as two hundred years or a hundred and fifty before the wars of David, but the actual time of writing may be coterminous between the two.

The story of David has many brutal warriors as well as an assortment of fools, liars, brave men, and devoted women, but it has only one great hero (unlike the *Iliad*) and it may be because Samuel and early Kings are not about a single great war or a great conquest but a study of the celebrated life and character, personality, and final weakness and even ugliness of the great figure, a warrior, a governor, and a poet, revered—in different ways—in all three Abrahamic religions. It could have been the study of the emergence of a great new nation, in which case the attention could have been to the endless battles and the guiding hand, and voice—of its God, which could have brought it a little closer to the *Iliad*, but, among other things, though there was great individual bravery, loyalty, and sacrifice, there is no real celebration of military prowess, for example, and no elevation to hero status of this or that brave Philistine or Israeli or Ammonite. The victory, and the losses, are David's and David's alone. Moab, a "field marshal" and a warrior the equal, say, of Ajax or even Hector, is given short shrift and is called a "field commander," about as important, it seems, as our Rommel or Patton. Whoever was the author of this epic, he devoted his attention, his great narrative, to the life of a shepherd king, to his singing, his political, managerial, and military skills, his assumption of power, his lusts, anger, religious obsession, remorse, grief, and sorrow. He—the author— was a psychologist, maybe one stuck in the tenth century BCE but superbly skilled in the mode and manner of royal behavior in archaic time, with the skill to penetrate, or create (or re-create), a complicated life, one with very little by way of a model to guide him through the travail. The only thing of Homer's which compares is that part of the life of Odysseus where his full humanity takes over, his great adventure, for example, in Phaeacia, where he pursues Nausicaa and attends to her parents, the king and queen, or in his ruthless desire to return to Ithaka, by any means. If someone named Homer was the poet here he shows—like the David narrator—an enormous understanding of warriors in the field, but the central fact is that the *Iliad* was the study of a war, whereas David (or Samuel) is the study of a primitive early king.

Harold Bloom, in his essay on *Hamlet*, "honors" David by saying that Hamlet, first and last, vies with King David and the Jesus of Mark as a charismatic of charismatics; he says that "Hamlet bears the Blessing, as David and Joseph and the wily Jacob." The Blessing is defined as "more life into a time without boundaries." It is also called "heroic vitalism." To Bloom, Hamlet is a "transcendental hero," a new kind of man—as David was. I thought of the gravedigger knocking his dirty shovel on the bare skulls and picking up the stripped head of Yorick, the king's jester. He—Yorick—was in the ground for twenty-three years (according to the text), and since Hamlet rode his shoulders as a small boy it indicates Hamlet's age as twenty-six or twenty-seven. I think a deliberate move by Shakespeare. We can't tell how the gravedigger knew it was Yorick and, more important, why the skull was loose like that in the dirt. My guess is he knew where everyone, certainly everyone of note, was buried, and that common people were just shoved in the hole with a minimum piece of wood or the early version of our cardboard to cover them. Alas, poor Yorick. It's of course a memory of the melancholic scholar with the death head on his blotter to remind him. This memory is there when Hamlet holds the skull up. *Memento mori.* I have to describe my own state, in this connection, as kind of objective, as if I both were and weren't participating. Or as if I were writing about someone else. I don't have a fever, I'm not depressed, and I am very attuned. Nor do I think it's a showpiece charade to actually take my mind off the subject, as one may think, though my mind is on the writing and the possibility of a different order in the writing and what might come next, which may itself—or themselves—be showpiece, as I describe it. I'm nervous about talking *about* the theme—if it's the theme—for I don't want to upset my children or my friends. When I somewhat shyly told Anne Marie I was thinking of buying a plot—maybe two—she reminded me that she wasn't Jewish. I said it didn't matter and she was too young anyhow to even consider the matter, but she was delighted by the offer even though, she said, I would just sing beside her forever, wouldn't I? And when I told my friend Judith Vollmer from Pittsburgh, she took it in naturally and told me—as everyone I've talked to—that she was going to get cremated, but also she thought of being buried with her family and the familiar bells began to ring.

At any rate, I saw that the terrain would be hard on me and I'd have to wait for a (younger) friend to lean on, even if I could drive my car through the grass and dirt almost to the section I wanted to see and walk through.

The Homestead Steel Strike

The famous Homestead Steel Strike—or lockout—occurred in 1892, one of the significant labor events of the
nineteenth and early twentieth centuries. The famous 11th
Encyclopaedia Britannica has an entry on Homestead in
which it is mentioned as if it were a rather insignificant
event, and not much attention is paid to the murderous
character of Henry Clay Frick, who managed Carnegie
Steel and succeeded finally in defeating the Amalgamated
Association of Iron and Steel Workers, the AA, through
corrupt political influence that resulted in the turning
out of the whole Pennsylvania State Guard to protect
strikebreakers and enforce a lockout of workers after a
reduction in wages, in spite of massive profits. Carnegie
himself, building little libraries in Scotland, always said
he was *for* unions, well, before *this* strike. Carnegie, the
Bearded Benevolent. Frick, on his deathbed, cried out (to
Carnegie): "I'll see you in Hell!"

Carnegie condemned the use of strikebreakers (in his writing), but he supported Frick in his desire to break the union. Frick built a high wooden fence topped with barbed wire around the Homestead Plant, with sniper towers, searchlights, and high-pressure water cannons at each entrance. Three hundred Pinkerton agents, armed with Winchester rifles, were towed up the Monongahela River in barges, intending to land at Homestead; but before they could, a battle ensued in which hundreds, even thousands, of armed Pittsburgh, Braddock, and Duquesne steelworkers supported the strikers. The townspeople—from Homestead—came out in force and occupied the mill.

It was the birth of what I later came to know as anarcho-syndicalism, the workers themselves running the plant, setting the rules, deciding the hours, the rate of production, and the like, for the managers were gone, as much for their own safety as anything. Except, since it was a strike—*and* a lockout—there was no production.

Practically the whole city of Homestead was at the plant. The fence was torn apart here and there to provide entrances into the mill. Whole families lay down on the bedding they had dragged in or, since it was a hot summer, many slept in the nearby fields or under the trees. Fires were started everywhere, and there were delicious bowls of cabbage and chicken soup, served with real spoons and big chunks of freshly baked bread. The children mostly sat cross-legged on the grass, but there were quite a few rough homemade tables and benches built by the idle workers for adults to sit on, constructed out of the plentiful lumber stored in sheds. There was a determined, even a grim, attitude on the part of the occupiers, for they knew there would be trouble ahead. But there was also a kind of party—or picnic—spirit, plenty of singing, accordion, and fiddle playing, and German, Irish, and Hungarian songs drifting through the trees. I remember one of the songs. It was sung in Czech but some of the children rendered it in English.

> Walking at night, along the village way,
> home from the dance beside my maiden gay.
> Walking at night, along the village way
> home from the dance beside my maiden gay.
> Stolla, stolla, stolla, pumpa
> Stolla pumpa, Stolla pumpa
> Stolla, stolla, stolla, pumpa
> Stolla pumpa pum, pum, pum.
>
> Nearing the wood, I heard a nightingale,
> softly it turned and sang its fairy tale.

Nearing the wood, I heard a nightingale,

softly it turned and sang its fairy tale.

Stolla, stolla, stolla, pumpa

Stolla pumpa, Stolla pumpa

Stolla, stolla, stolla, pumpa

Stolla pumpa pum, pum, pum.

The workers fired at the barges with a twenty-pound brass cannon and engaged in rifle fire with the Pinkertons, resulting in dozens of people being killed or wounded. The workers tried to set the barges on fire by floating burning rafts downriver and setting the river itself on fire by pouring oil on the water and lighting it. The Pinkertons finally hoisted a white flag, but when they landed they were forced to run a gauntlet where men, women, and children threw sand and stones at them, spit on them, and beat them. The women, it was noted in the *New York Times*, were especially ferocious, and the Pinkerton agents were terrified. They were finally driven to Pittsburgh, then freed. The Amalgamated Association tried desperately to get Frick back to the table but he stubbornly refused. When the governor ordered the militia to Homestead, they protected the strikebreakers, and very soon the mill was in full production. And when Alexander Berkman attempted to assassinate Frick (and merely wounded him), public opinion shifted. Both sides accused the other of being "anarchists," the word at the time for terrorists. It wasn't till the 1930s that the steelworkers were able—through federal law—to organize. Throughout the intervening time the Carnegies and the Fricks had a free hand.

Emma Goldman

Emma Goldman, for whom there is no stamp, was born in 1885 and twenty-three years old in 1908 when she—and her lover Alexander Berkman—planned the assassination of Henry Clay Frick. Berkman took a train to Pittsburgh, shot Frick three times, and stabbed him in the leg, but Frick survived. Berkman was convicted of attempted murder and sentenced to twenty-two years in prison. My heart goes out to him. I know how mean and nasty the police can be. Mean, nasty, and stupid. They humiliated and punished him endlessly for attempting to murder a great bastard, an abuser and exploiter par excellence, one who, in effect, forced his underpaid workers to contribute handsomely to the purchase of great works of art, which now adorn the walls of museums that are named after the prick himself, may he burn in an open hearth furnace forever, may his feet catch on fire first, then his blistered hands, and his dumb face. But the police know nothing about this. They are trained to beat up vagrants, to distribute tickets, to take their small hats off to bigger hats. In Berkman's case he was chained to a wall for a year. His privileges were taken away; he was starved.

If in Pittsburgh you were a subversive of any kind, the police, like smart dogs, smelled you out. In my case, as I have written elsewhere many times, I was smelled out, and though I wasn't chained, I was handcuffed—on a false charge—and accused of being a Communist because, as I said earlier, I went to a Henry Wallace meeting and was accused of being a rapist because I was standing on a certain bridge at one a.m., both the very same night. I don't want to murder anyone, because my political sentiments don't lie that way, but the legal penalty for attempted murder (Berkman's "crime") was seven years—at the time—not twenty-two. Though he did get out after fourteen. The view now is that Berkman was only a tool for Goldman and a mere addendum. But he was respected and loved in his own right. He died in 1936, a suicide, in Nice, France, after two failed operations and after a lifetime of disappointment, suffering, and hard work.

Goldman was harassed by the police, but they found no evidence against her. What the two of them did was called "propaganda of the deed." Emma Goldman, who died in 1940, was called "the most dangerous woman in America" by J. Edgar Hoover who, himself, was certainly the most dangerous man in America. She was deeply moved by the Haymarket Rebellion, and it, along with the Homestead Lockout, remained her touchstones. Vivian Gornick, writing about Goldman, referenced her passionate personal involvement in the political positions she took, as opposed to an alternative ideological, or *merely* ideological, involvement. She was more therefore like an artist—a poet—in her presentation of a position; and she reminds us of the Jewish prophets in their outrage and outrageous behavior when it came to the matters that were important to them. It was in fact out of this prophetic tradition that both she and Berkman came, and it was no accident that they both were Jews, however lapsed and secular they were. Indeed it was the mostly Jewish world of the Lower East Side—and Sachs's Café in particular—from which so many activities of the left, from Social Democrats to Socialists to Anarchists, sprang. During her most popular time, Emma Goldman spoke to four or five thousand people gathered together in Union Square at 14th Street to thunderous acclaim. She traveled the nation and made dozens of appearances in lecture halls in Cleveland, Detroit, Philadelphia, and Denver; in

San Diego and Los Angeles; in Oakland, Milwaukee, and Seattle; demanding decent pay, equal rights for women, the eight-hour day, and respect and justice for the working person as well as the right to organize. At the same time, she blasted governments—all governments—and practically cursed gradualism. She made friends with labor leaders and politicians of the left, such as Eugene Debs. But they were temporary alliances for she was in favor of something immediate, and she broke bread with leaders of the IWW and the "native" Socialists in the Midwest and West Coast, in the strangest of all marriages, between Ohio and Nebraska Protestants brought up on John Locke and Thomas Jefferson and Millennial John on the one hand and Yiddish, Russian, and German speakers brought up on Nietzsche, Bakunin, and Isaiah on the other.

She was seen—by the tabloids—as a "property-destroying, capitalist-killing, riot-promoting agitator" (Nellie Bly, the *New York World*) who delivered "wild blood-thirsty harangues" and spent a year on Blackwell's Island (middle of the East River) for inciting to riot—when she was only twenty-four. At first she delivered her speeches in German, but while in prison she taught herself English. She was world-famous, Red Emma, in every city in Europe and North America. Berkman was released after his fourteen years in jail and they reunited. A decade or so later they organized protests against the Conscription Act of 1917 as America was readying itself for its entry into the First World War, and thousands joined their protest. In one case, 2,000 people were crowded inside a hall and an estimated 35,000 were outside (Cooper Union, the Harlem River Casino, and dozens of other venues). Emma and Sasha (Berkman) were arrested and charged with conspiracy to obstruct the draft. At their trial, they each spoke in their own defense. Vivian Gornick called Emma's speech the "soapbox of her dreams." Her position was that of a conscientious objector, and what she said could be summed up in one of her sentences: "The righteous passion for justice can never express itself in human slaughter." She invoked Jesus, Socrates, Galileo, the Founding Fathers, and the Abolitionists. She called them "the anarchists of their time." She and Berkman were found guilty and sentenced to two years, she to Missouri, Berkman to Atlanta, where he was kept for months in an underground dungeon for protesting against the brutalities practiced against other inmates. This particular hole was four and a half feet by two and a half feet and too small to stand up in. He spent almost his entire time there, and when he was released he was a broken man. When they left prison, they, along with hundreds of others, were deported, to Russia in their case, called by its new name, the USSR. They were deported for their *opinions*, their thoughts, and their writings. With the good help of Tsar J. Edgar, the patriotic consumer of cottage cheese. They didn't last long in Russia either, for anarchists and Communists are weird bedfellows (party power vs. worker control). When they left Russia, they went from country to country but were always permitted only a short stay. England admitted them, but when they spoke against the Soviets, they were banned by such writers as H. G. Wells, Bertrand Russell, and Havelock Ellis.

Goldman, in the mid-1920s, grieved over the state murders of Sacco and Vanzetti and the repetitions of the injustices surrounding the Haymarket rebellion in the late 1880s, less than forty years earlier. She finally found the occasion to celebrate, if only for a little, when the workers in Spain, in the mid-1930s, were able to create a genuine "worker's state"—at least in Catalonia, Aragon, and Andalusia—where they were in control for a short time during the civil war before the Fascists, together with the Stalinists, destroyed them.

Emma Goldman spent her last years in Canada. She had married a Welsh anarchist by the name of James

Colton and went by his last name. She longed to return to the United States but was not permitted. Goldman died in Toronto, in 1940, at the age of seventy. The U.S. permitted her body to be returned to America, where she was buried among the graves of those executed after the Haymarket affair.

It is hard—in 2014—to categorize Goldman, even to fully understand her. She was an anarchist when anarchism was well known, popular, and still believable. There were hundreds, thousands, of anarchists in Europe and North America. It was probably the most popular leftist position, and there were anarchists of this and that stripe, Italian anarchists, and Russian and Jewish and Spanish and French and American. She was also a writer of the first order and a major orator and spoke to thousands, in dozens of cities. She spoke German, Russian, Yiddish, English, and French. Well to perfectly. She was befriended by Peggy Guggenheim, and her publisher considered asking Herbert Hoover to write the introduction to her autobiography. She was not strictly a feminist, as feminism was understood during her lifetime. She was more interested in erotic love than she was in women's suffrage. She certainly favored women's participation in all things, but, as an anarchist, she couldn't be much moved by the

vote. It was the eight-hour day, unions, decent wages, em-
ployee self-governance, and justice that moved her, above
all, a woman's control—in all ways—of her own body
that she spoke for. It goes without saying that she was
pro-abortion and for birth control, but it was primarily
sexual fulfillment and love that motivated her. They called
it "free love" for a while, and it went hand in hand with
their revolutionary ideas. The commune of the 1960s was
a born-again idea. It was sexual radicalism; though often
confused and confounded. Goldman had many affairs,
each a repetition of the former, almost a religious devotion to sexual passion. And she deeply connected it with
politics. Love was the essence of both. Anarchic love. She
is the spine of this book.

Mt. Hope Again

I was always near a river, and that was something. The earth was rich and clean, unless we had labored there, and there were always valleys embracing the river and steep hills beyond. First it was the Allegheny and the Mononga-hela—and the Ohio twisting north and south—but I guess I was more loyal to the Allegheny, the Sixth Street Bridge and all, the river towns up north and the great forests; then the Hudson, more like the Mississippi, that; then, in my twenties the Seine—where poets drowned—and the Arno, where I rowed a boat and walked across the old bridge; and then the lower Delaware at Philadelphia and twenty years later the beautiful upper where I lived on the banks for thirteen years; the Susquehanna next, and that meant all three systems in Pennsylvania; and for a while—for fourteen years—the Iowa; and now the Delaware again, the eastern bank. And I was so near the two canals, Pennsylvania and New Jersey, the D&R—that I half-think

my great and greater-great Ukrainian fathers were poling
boats and whispering to the stubborn mules instead of
farming fish and growing leaf in their few hectares north
a piece from Kiev, and praising God at fixed hours, though
watchless, and going inside at last to the smoky rooms and
dirt floors of their small houses where everything know-
able had a word for it in the thirteenth-century German
they spoke—called Yiddish—and Russian to the goyim,
sometimes who loved them and sometimes raised crude
instruments against them.

Mt. Hope looks down on the whole river valley. Some
stones (grave markers) are—were—so old that they were
replaced, with the same dates of course, and the same
sentiments. A close study can tell you a lot about the
history—the early names, the religious persuasions. The
small Jewish section has only one stone at this time, Rabbi
Sandy. If I choose to go there, I could be one of the earliest.
Depending, naturally. Anne Marie says I would want to be
close to the rabbi to continue my flirtation. So I wouldn't
just be singing. I don't know what the earth smells like
there. I think the drainage is good, given the hill, so there
won't be much water.

The closest I came to facing pure dirt was when I
created for myself a kind of study two cellars down in an

ancient house on Limekiln Pike in West Oak Lane in Philadelphia where we lived in the early 1960s. There were tiny steps, more a wooden ladder down into the sub-cellar, and the space was about seven feet by ten. The walls were earth as well as the floor, and there were the ends of roots sticking out as well as shiny miniscule stones. You let yourself in through a trapdoor. There was a chopping block there, the only piece of furniture, which I guessed, because of the carving and the design, was from the early part of the nineteenth century, 1810 or '20. I used the maple top for a writing surface and brought down a kitchen chair and disentangled the very long red extension cord and hung the bright light on a spike I pounded into the hard dirt. It was absolutely silent down there, no distractions, and I wrote and read undisturbed. It was one of the best studies I ever had. I had some hair then, though not much, and a moustache and horn-rimmed glasses. I was more or less content with my life, very happy on occasion, with my former wife and my two small children, whom I adored. I was fairly poor—by any standard—but we seemed to eat well, and part of the reason that we didn't lack much is that we didn't desire a lot. I had a 1950 Chevy—strip in the windshield—and we only bought an ancient television set from a more or less blind friend for twenty-five dollars so we could watch Kennedy's inauguration. Sometimes I wanted to be in France or Italy, or California, but I never obsessed about it, nor did I in any way feel trapped nor was I nostalgic for the life I *didn't* live, nor did I want to exchange my hole in the ground for a more lofty place. I never thought I was buried there. Even if it had the aspect of a grave about it. Which caused me, from time to time, to consider whether an electric wire, a lightbulb, a kitchen chair, and a chopping block were enough to take with me into the next world, plus pen and paper. No frying pan? or knife? or an egg or two, or a blanket? For such a voyage, when I smelled the earth around me and saw the mica flicks in my low-lying atmosphere, the humor of it, and the terror, were never far from my mind.

Shoshana, the International Writing Program

I'll say only this by way of identification, that S. was an Israeli in the International Writing Program, the IWP, at the University of Iowa, about 1990, while I was teaching there at the Writers' Workshop; that she traveled to Poland with her father I think in the early 1980s and he, discovering his old street, his house even, sat down on the wooden steps and wept and, for a short time, lost his mind, and never fully recovered.

The writers, from China, Brazil, Russia, the Congo, arrived by plane at the end of August and stayed through Thanksgiving. They argued, read, and wrote, and then they visited a major city, New Orleans, San Francisco, New York. I met S. at the orientation party, but I was tied up with this and that all during their residency and didn't see her again till late in November just before they were leaving, at a lecture of some kind, where we sat side by side, I on the left. I was intensely moved by her, though I didn't expect anything to happen. I wasn't looking for it, I didn't especially want it. It was as if it happened against my better judgment, even against my wishes. I was probably sixty-five, she forty-seven or so. We spent the next few evenings together and ended up one night in the front seat of my car in a park by the river kissing each other like crazy teenagers. A uniformed policeman pulled up quietly alongside us, and when he saw—with the aid of a flashlight—that we, certainly that I, was along in years, he apologized and suggested it was dangerous there, but he didn't say "inappropriate." The policeman could have been my son's age and the sight may have been shocking, certainly unexpected, to him.

I think it was the next night, her last in Iowa before she left for New York and then home, that we went to my house for a small bite. I had written her a letter—by hand—late that afternoon and gave it to her, maybe a little reluctantly, after we ate. She took the letter into the living room, sat down in an armchair, and read it, probably at least twice. I tried in the letter to explain my cautiousness—she was leaving the next day, the other end of the world—and though I had a strong desire for her, we might not see each other ever again, which wouldn't be fair to either of us. But she came into the kitchen, where I was cleaning up and said, "You've won me with words; let's go upstairs." I was surprised and delighted. We made love, a little too quickly for me for I knew we would have to get up again, in the cold, after the few hours allotted to us. "Stay up," I said, almost aloud, "she is leaving tomorrow," and the next instant, I woke up to the light, having slept the last night through.

She had a huge metal suitcase, practically a trunk, in her apartment, which we filled in no time with sheets, towels, nightgowns, hair dryers, electric toothbrushes, soaps and unguents, sandals, blouses, underwear, hair-brushes, *und so weiter*, all from K-Mart, when they opened at ten a.m.—maybe it was nine, for her plane was leaving at eleven. Her mind, it seemed to me, was on her purchases, as she pulled me from place to place; my mind was on her. As my desire converted to deep affection. Call it love—why not? I saw her two or three times since then and we talked by phone. She had gotten a brutal divorce. She was arriving in New York with her sixteen-year-old daughter. We were due to meet at a bakery she knew—half bakery, half coffee shop. She was worried that her daughter hadn't eaten the whole day. Fear of anorexia. Jewish mother fears. I saw her differently, but my affection only deepened with her anxiety. Then I saw her once more in

America and twice in her country. Every time we met she would tell me how amazed she was that I once had loved her—or showed such affection. I saw her four years ago. She had become a famous writer. She bought me lunch in a lovely restaurant. When I asked her about the men in her life, she deflected the question; nothing intimate, only need, men—in her country—weren't worth it. They were selfish babies, etc. The sea was nearby. Shoshana.

Shoshana, Hotel Earle

Whenever I visit someone at the Washington Square Hotel, in the Village off the square on the way to Sixth Avenue, I am reminded—with great pleasure—of the hotel that once occupied the space and was known as the Hotel Earle. The Washington Square is a famous "boutique" hotel, which means that the room is little larger than the bed itself and the bed—at its largest—is a double or a "matrimonial," the name it was given in the Latin countries, where beds were important locations for sickness, dying, and breeding; but, given the stinginess in voltage, hardly a place for either a pen or a book, at least to my knowledge and memory. The Earle I used to always stay at when I visited New York, and I love to torture the young with descriptions of it, and watch them die with amazement and envy. There were two very decent-sized rooms in every case: a full-sized bedroom, with bed, closet, wardrobe, desk, and the other accoutrements, a

nice bathroom and a full living—or sitting—room with
sofa, chairs, tables, lamps, and the like. The rooms, a little
dusty, were heated by steam, and the radiators, in the cold
months, were always hot and noisy—I must have stayed
there fifteen or twenty times in the 1950s and '60s, and I
even considered seriously moving there where the nightly
rental was seven dollars and the monthly rental, I think,
a hundred and twenty-five, much more expensive than a
furnished room or a cold-water flat, but after all a hotel,
with all the services and attention. Though during the
1970s it became a welfare hotel, as did many other me-
dium- and low-priced hotels, with the costs borne by the
city, or the state, or God knows whom. By then I had a four-
room walk-through apartment on Vandam Street west of
Sixth in the northern reaches of Soho and had given up on
the Earle, so I wasn't aware of the deterioration that had
occurred. Nor was I particularly aware of the money crisis
in the city, or who the mayor was and how he had gathered
harm, like shiny seeds, into his flimsy basket, and where
he was distributing it. I hardly read the *Times*, I had no
TV, and I was struggling with my own life and the words
that consumed me. And I had young children and a house
two hours away in Pennsylvania, and a job in New Jersey
an hour away, give and take some.

I brought a woman into the city, but for some reason or other my apartment wasn't available, so I had to look for a place for our weary heads and thought of the old Earle where I had stayed so many times. When we entered the minuscule lobby there was no one there at the desk and only when the attendant opened the ancient elevator was I aware that one person doubled, nay tripled, as desk clerk, elevator operator, and bellhop. He was wearing a short-sleeve—dirty—smock with his black and gray chest hairs sticking out of the openings between the buttons since he wasn't wearing an undershirt, neither T nor wife-beater. Moreover, the smock was too small and threatened to pop the buttons at any minute. He showed deep surprise at our being there, and I became immediately aware that it wasn't, as such, a "public" hotel but one underwritten by government funds, which I had heard about—or read—somewhere, a "welfare" hotel. Nevertheless he showed us a room upstairs—two connected rooms. I thought it was dirtier than it formerly was, and there were black flecks on the window sills, but we were happy we had a place. Though when we went into the bedroom we saw water coming out of a pipe above the bed as well as a cracked window with the wind blowing through. It was an intermittent—and small—flow of water but enough to make the bedclothes damp, wet I'd say, or somewhere in between, so that she—or I—lying on that side of the bed, would be more than a little discomfited, whatever stage of affection we were in. Moreover, she had burst into tears, whether it was from the chest hairs or the wet bed, an excess of emotion, which struck me at the time as somewhat inappropriate for a thirty-eight- or thirty-nine-year-old woman, the mother of four. It ruined our idyll at the Earle, nor did I even want to see another apartment, for who knows what fresh horror we would encounter. I gave the button popper a twenty, which would adequately cover the seven dollars, if that was what it still was, or even if the price had gone up to ten or fifteen, not that I was a sport, I just didn't want to see the asshole again.

What we did was venture out into the early dark, and I called a friend of mine who had an apartment nearby, which she let us use, since she was away somewhere. So—after we found the key—we ended up having an idyll anyway, even if it was in a bunk bed (I remember), in a very small, heavily overheated room. Which I remember not because of the great passion there but because I associate that venture always with the welfare hotel and the three-headed gatekeeper, something out of Greek mythology, a Cerberus who ran an old-fashioned elevator, carried your bags, and registered you in the big book of guests, a separate function to go with each of the three heads. Her name, even her initials, I'll keep to myself since she lives nearby and called me up out of the blue one Sunday morning recently—to congratulate me on a poem I'd published or to relive a little of that time, though I never for a minute mentioned the Hotel Earle to her, the wet bed, or the broken window, maybe out of kindness, maybe I just didn't think of it. Shoshana.

Shoshana, Marie

There was a woman whose first name was Marie I used to see from time to time when I was nineteen or twenty years old and a student at the University of Pittsburgh. She was, I'd say, in her mid-forties and had a son my age, also a college student; there was a man who used to sit at the far end of her long front porch she referred to as her "uncle," but whom I was absolutely sure was her husband, who not only tolerated her infidelities but was undoubtedly stimulated—if that was the word then—adding a peculiar complication, a kind of seasoning to my friendship with Marie. He must have seen me a number of times—as I saw him—ringing the bell to the front door, but he never left his chair to talk to me. I know I was not charged by seeing him, as I know that he didn't enter—as a participant—in any way into our relationship, Marie and I, at least not from my side, though it might possibly have been from hers. Something perverse, and dark, I might have said then, though it seems to me something simple and easy to explain from my present perch. What *was* dark and perverse was me visiting Marie, twice my age and, I think, more or less my mother's age. Any eighth-grade psychologist would have a field day with that, but I knew, even then, that sex was various and that in the underbelly of our culture a lot, a huge amount, goes on that is not accounted for or only hinted at. Today's porn hardly touches the forbidden. It is, essentially, a *fake* forbidden, as false as the yells and moans of its participants. A camera cannot easily record the dark and perverse.

Reading, hearsay, and a little experience taught me all this. Different cultures behave differently, and since our connection—Marie and I—gave me much pleasure and knowledge I pursued it with aplomb, for its own sake, for I knew, sane and proper as I was, that it was only temporary and destined to be short-lived. In a certain way, although it was I who rang the bell, it was nonetheless I who was the Susanna and that there was a full-fledged reversal of gender roles, though I was certainly not bathing and caught unawares by lusty and greedy voyeurs, and I was in no position to write a memoir, say, of how I was outraged and preyed upon, for I wasn't. Marie struggled with the forbidden. She loved it, in a way. Sometimes there *was* a light knock on the door of the downstairs room where we made love, and she pulled me over, an inch away from the door but unseen as she poked her head out and engaged in light talk and banter with the young lady, probably my age, who rented a room upstairs—while she touched me, aroused as I was, for three or four minutes before she said goodbye and closed the door, a three-way thing where only one of the parties had the knowledge yet all three participated in their diverse ways. In her own quiet manner she controlled everything; and it was her sexual imagination, however it was grounded, wherever it came from, that determined levels of action as if it were a Niebelung or a Danse Russe she was conducting. I went to school there, bad student that I was. Shoshana.

Shoshana, Greece

Minor poets borrow, major ones steal, said T. S. E., something like that, but is it a major act to steal from yourself, or to steal just a little? Something even your self would hardly notice? And can you make a minor change or two, connecting, or enlarging, on the experience? Is that minor or major?

I was going south on a subway late at night, an A or a C, destination Vandam Street, subway stop Houston, when we bypassed or skipped the station, continued south to Canal (since they were repairing something) and "crossed over" to wait for a northbound train to Houston, four or five of us. I proposed a cab but the others were suspicious, so after waiting for a half-hour we got into a slow-moving and noisy "repair" car. A young woman got off the subway with me and we both made our way south, me trying not to "follow" her, she frozen with fear. While still walking I told her my name was Gerald Stern, I lived on the next street, and I meant her no harm. To which she replied: "My God, I'm just home from Greece—the Aegean School in Paros. I was told to look you up." I don't know why she was heading down Varick, but she ended up coming to my apartment on Vandam. I gave her some food, we talked for two hours, and she ended up sleeping there. She lived uptown in Inwood, 190th Street. She came by to see me once or twice more. She was doing some kind of commercial art—maybe she was a clothes designer, and she also wrote poetry, which brought her to Paros in the first place and to my apartment on Vandam Street, five flights up.

It was the late 1980s, I remember, so I was in my early sixties. She was in her early thirties, the age—I think—of half the young women in New York in the arts: writing, acting, painting, and I guess she had a nervous family somewhere west or south, maybe southwest. Let me only say that she had a very beautiful body, that frightened deer who was cornered by a very hungry coyote; and that it was the closest thing to the actual Susanna at her bath, for she indeed stepped into my orange-colored bathtub, in the kitchen of course, and used a large sponge to wash herself, which she had brought back from Greece, home of sponges and ancient marble fragments with bright-colored nymphs painted on the curved surfaces. And that even then I luxuriated as one of the elders, closer than they of the myth, and grateful to the book of Daniel for the honor. Shoshana.

D. P.'s

Sometimes I let the very tip of my pen do the thinking for
me, and sometimes I sit in a chair going over things before
I pick up a Marriot plume or even a Bic itself to register
my thoughts. I was both and neither today, December 21,
2013, a full moon laying it on, the temperature in the upper
forties, night arriving at the unseemly hour of 4:30. It was
the initials D. P. and the words "displaced persons" I was
thinking of as, for one reason or another, I was remembering the years after World War II, 1945–1950, and what
the lives of D. P.'s were in those years, refugees—refuse—
mostly from Eastern Europe, and the "temporary" camps
they were lodged in, and what their hopes were, and now,
how the words, the initials, have become a metaphor for
our general condition today of displacement, and what I
am making of it in my own life and what my experience of
it was, both literal and figurative.

Displacement, the act of moving something from its

original place to a new—and uncomfortable—place. I say "original," for displacement occurs only when there is an original place. The D. P.'s were nationals of one kind or another who couldn't return to the original place since that place lost its meaning, or no longer existed in the same way, or just no longer existed. Baltic nationals were displaced as the Russians took over; Jews who survived extermination were displaced. Romanians, Hungarians, Slovaks, Poles.

But though I am deeply interested in the politically displaced, I am equally, or more, interested in displacement as a general human condition in our time—and in my life—economically, psychologically, philosophically. True believer to atheist (and why not atheist to believer); country mouse to city mouse; some kind of discontinuity and rupture, not always bad. Even a source of creativity (*one* of the sources), our best artists, our musicians, our writers, overwhelmed by displacement. Technology and displacement. Discontinuity. Not only are refugees subject to displacement (or objects of displacement) but immigrants themselves. My mother and father, struggling with the old language, abandoning, for the most part, the religion, subjecting themselves—eagerly—to the new culture. Living in fake nostalgia. Hardly remembering the names of the boats; forgetting their (last) goishe language, and is not to sleep with Murphy, to not have a single wall, or a desk, or a bookcase, or a closet, or a dresser, to be a D. P.? Neither "mad Ireland" nor madder America drove me into poetry. I could have been a rug buyer or a social worker or a labor lawyer. I really was all three. And isn't it the greatest displacement of all that waits for us?

We will be refugees, mythic Ukrainians and Estonians, Jews, impoverished, sick, enflooded, oil-ridden, and bombed and homeless; and stateless, our quaint mud street taken over by ideologues and land-hungry vermin, who made no bones about it, who sat on our faces, who cut our fingers off and sometimes our noses and set our haystacks on fire and forced their languages on us, not to mention their greedy religions, and redrew the boundaries and remade the history and hardly allotted us protein enough and forced us to live where water could drown us for we were in a valley and it was called the valley of hopelessness and the valley of dread; and as for the larger picture, not one of us will have enough money for the return, not one of us will even remember.

Of all people, of all poets, it is Emily Dickinson who, to my knowledge, first mentions the word "refugee" in a poem, seventy-five years before Auden used it in another poem. Here is Dickinson's poem, four lines:

These Strangers, in a Foreign world
Protection asked of me —
Befriend them, lest yourself in Heaven
Be found a Refugee —

It is no. 1094, or 1096, depending on which collection you use. I'm not sure who the refugees were in her poem, Irish maybe (it was New England) or possibly blacks; Auden's were Jewish, but I don't know if there were Jews in Amherst in 1864 and—if there were—whether they were seen as refugees, and the "huddled masses" wasn't written yet. Except that Jews are always displaced persons. Certainly during the last two thousand years. Earlier even. Displaced, exiled, always to one degree or other homeless, even if they don't sleep on cardboard, even if they do—some of them—live in mansions. And they—we— disagree, sometimes violently, about what homelessness means. In a hundred ways; in a thousand.

Me, I married out of the religion, I took my son and daughter to Sunday school in a college town I lived and worked in, but sporadically; I didn't join the synagogue or go to services. I made a half-assed attempt to have my son bar-mitzvahed but it went nowhere, my daughter became a Christian and my son married an Irish girl, my grandchildren probably haven't the vaguest idea of who or what a Jew is, my daughter probably taught her children some Christian nonsense about Jews, if anything; my mother and father, born in Europe, were the youngest, spoke English without an accent and argued in Yiddish, and my mother was depressed and, after my sister died—at nine—wasn't able to take care of a household. We lived in a small apartment, with one bedroom, the three of us, and I slept on either a Murphy bed (as I said) or a couch in the living room. I didn't have either a desk or a dresser (as I said), let alone a bookcase, or a wall for posters. I had no place to put anything, even my socks and underwear—it was as if I weren't there—and I had no privacy. My father, notwithstanding, made a large salary and we always had a new, or recent, car, ate in restaurants, and had a full-time sleep-in maid. Judaism in our lives was mostly seen in terms of anti-Semitism. We had no books or magazines, we lived in a roiling sea of schmaltz and nostalgia and never exchanged true ideas. I don't think I ever did one night's homework. I lived mostly in a pool hall when I wasn't at school and spent hundreds of hours by myself, walking or reading. I was an adult at fourteen, physically and emotionally, and went my own way. I always worked for my money and rather tolerated my parents—as children—yet I loved them and felt responsible. I was more than displaced. I was de-placed, and my own dream was that I had my own room, a desk, and books, and lived in a small city up north, and went to some third-rate college or other but was my own man. I always saw to it, when I had my own children, that they would each have their own place—their own room, no matter how poor I was. That came before anything else.

I was not happy, at the time, with many of the D. P.'s for though they were refugees, some of them, they were so because of their political preferences rather than their helplessness as a result of their persecution; some from the Baltic countries, some from Ukraine. The Lithuanians were about to be overwhelmed again by the Russians, only this time the Rooskies went by the name of "communist." The Jewish population in Lithuania was decimated, as was that in Estonia and Latvia. Those countries found it convenient, in their "anti-communism," to side with the Germans and participated in the destruction of the Jewish population, in Vilna, for example. America freely admitted them, without a very sophisticated understanding of their position. I met quite a few over the years who were pro-German and, of course, deeply anti-Semitic. But all of Europe had a "Jewish problem," and almost every country was steadfastly opposed to the return of the Jews, those who survived. Europe itself, the whole continent, was deeply sick, Catholic Europe, Protestant Europe, secular. And it has gotten complicated—again—with the emergence of Israel and its mistreatment of the Arab Palestinians. Europe, the greediest, most imperial, most self-congratulatory, for over four, five, centuries, has become extremely righteous in regard to Jewish nationalism, as if Zionism were not grounded in the European experience, in Europe. I was in France when the French were butchering Algerians, and I vividly remember the English creation ex nihilo of the Mau-Mau, cannibals, savages, and, of course, black. Not to mention America and its imperialism, in Chile, Venezuela, Panama, Cuba, Nicaragua, Guatemala, Puerto Rico, the Philippines, and, yes, Vietnam. Goddamn Europe and Goddamn what we learned from Europe, we Americans. And Goddamn Lithuania and the revival of anti-Semitism in Europe. Goddamn France in particular and Goddamn Francis if he permits the sanctification of Pope Pius, he who made Jews he was "protecting" come daily to mass, he who never even excommunicated Adolf Hitler. And Goddamn American Capitalism and God bless the homeless. And give them long coats.

Transgressive Behavior

I am given to excessive "explaining" of my own life and even have a certain pride, or at least pleasure, in what Anne Marie, who has heard everything—and more—calls "transgressive behavior." "Criminality lite," I'd call it. And I made a list of my transgressions on a small Blooming-dale's card, that of a salesperson there whose name was Jean that I pulled from my wallet though why it was there in the first place I have no idea. Transgressions I call "lite" though in theological tracts they are associated with what is called "sin," which I suppose makes then much more serious, and also associated with disobedience, Adam's sin, and rebellion, a subdivision of disobedience. Though rebellion, in our day, is not just chewing on an apple, it is for the sake of something, justice and such, unless it is the quaint rebellion "without a cause" the 1950s were famous for, even if there was a cause staring you in the face—or sitting on your chest. In one religion we beg the Lord for forgiveness of our transgression even as we forgive those who transgress against us. A version of the Lord's Prayer, so-called by Paul and offered by Jesus in two of the versions, an ancient Jewish prayer though I was advised by my rabbi to keep my mouth shut in elementary school while it was recited at the morning cleansing.

My transgressions were at bottom comic, and I knew I was committing a comic (if serious) act at the time of their doing, beginning in the sixth grade, when I was eleven. I went to a school called Colfax, and the principal's name was Miss Shepherd. My homeroom teacher was Miss Donaldson, four foot eleven and redheaded. She explained gravity by bouncing a small red rubber ball on the floor, and before the Lord's Prayer, the Pledge of Allegiance, and the Bible reading she made all the boys in the class hold out their hands to be hit by a strap. There was a small auditorium at the school, and we went there one day to watch a cartoonist (from the *Pittsburgh Press*) draw cartoons on the stage and explain the art. Someone had to run up, grab one of the cartoons, and run out of the room. I remember the cartoonist's name was Cy Hungerford; and I was chosen. In Miss Shepherd's office, a little later in the day, she was getting ready to hit me with a huge paddle, with large holes in the wood I guess for the pain, and suddenly her wig fell off and there she was, bald. "I won't spank you," she said, "if you don't tell anyone." Naturally I promised, but it was the talk of the school the next day.

This was the beginning, more or less, of my transgressive behavior. It was followed by other junior high and high school pranks and continued through my adult years. Just now the phone rang and a thing called Amy congratulated me in a euphoric voice, on winning a free trip to the Bahamas, business bullshit, abusing me and Amy simultaneously, true trespassing, but there are two or three wild squirrels running through the snow in my backyard and that calms me down. When I was in Rome with Patricia, in my mid-twenties, I took the time to piss voluminously on Titus's Arch, planted there to commemorate the destruction of Jerusalem and the ingathering of Jewish slaves. Transgressive, that. And I took a long slow bath during a party at a friend's house, the hostess sitting on the edge of the tub sponging my back, while her husband fretted with the other guests. And I lay down on Walt's bed in Camden (to talk to Oscar Wilde) while a friend of mine distracted the gatekeeper with questions, downstairs in the backyard; and I stole W. C. W.'s old straw hat (which fit me perfectly) and replaced it with my own during a visit to the small library and the poet's "office"—pipe, dictionary, and all—down the street from his house in Rutherford. And at Rowan College, in southern New Jersey, in a museum-like room where LBJ and Brezhnev held a top-level meeting, I was interviewed by Bill Moyers—after a Dodge Poetry Festival in the late 1980s—and wrote in Johnson's little notebook, on display with his ashtray and pen, a little note, "Shouldn't we bomb the Rooskies," which I'm sure historians have puzzled over. Both American and Rooskie historians. That was absolutely pure transgressive behavior. It just comes to me—as things come to comedians. And I saw my own activism, such as it was, as a type of theater, or circus, where I was simultaneously a slack-rope walker, a juggler, and a clown, a friend at court of Abbie Hoffman and Ginsberg, though Allen was not given to that type of irony, except in his Prague incarnation. The humor I brought to the individual act was expressed as double vision, distance, and even a kind of hopelessness.

Among other things, I defeated a Dean of Men who wanted to censor a publication I was the faculty advisor to; I single-handedly protested the building of a brick wall across the street in the southern reaches of Temple University in Philadelphia, which, nominally, marked the border but whose real purpose was to keep out the African Americans in whose ghetto Temple was located. I did it by climbing over the six-foot wall, necktie, briefcase, and all, as my way of going to work as an instructor there, followed after a while by fifteen or so others, mostly graduate students, till the wall was finally removed, the bricks piled up for a few weeks. I publicly and vociferously lectured the president of that college at a meeting of the whole faculty where he had just addressed us on the "philosophy of salaries at Temple," pointing out his rhetorical and usage errors (since I was an "English" teacher), for which my goose was cooked (all of this and more following I wrote about elsewhere). And I helped integrate the "public" swimming pool in Indiana, Pennsylvania, by jumping in one Sunday afternoon with a dark friend who had a PhD in economics from Harvard and who taught with me at Indiana University of Pennsylvania, a segregated town owned by coal barons, where Jimmy Stewart once lived and whose Oscars were displayed in Stewart's Hardware on the main thoroughfare, Philadelphia Street. And I organized and led a march in that town in memory of the boys murdered in Mississippi, the largest march in Pennsylvania, by "manipulating" the conservative clergy, the state police, and the college administration through a few acts of distortion. And I led a group called LOLA (Leave Our Land Alone) who were protesting the conversion of our little back road on the Delaware River in Raubsville, Pennsylvania, to a recreational zone (my old stone house turned into a canoe ramp). And won by forcing a yea or nay vote for the county commissioners up on the stage for immediate recall. And I orchestrated a rally to divest from South Africa at the University of Iowa, which led the very next day to divestment by all the largest colleges in the state. And at the community college where I taught for thirteen years before going to Iowa, I half-ran the school and, as head of the union, spoke Yiddish and French at the negotiations table and made secret deals with the board chairman and the attorney who opposed me at the table, unbeknownst to the administration and the faculty, which brought us amazing results both in salary and conditions of work— all with a secret delight that came more out of the Marx Brothers than it did out of the great Karl. And even at my own court-martial—in 1946—where I changed my plea (to innocent of all charges) at the last minute, much to my own attorney's surprise and chagrin, causing a kind of confusion in the room and putting me somehow in control, there was a comic devil-may-care element. This governed most of my public acts; from putting my quarter in the meter to meeting God on the road, generally a wind-swept weed-strewn empty one (I mean the road, not God). It was as if Jimmy Durante or Mel Brooks were president, not Obama or either of the (poison-berry) Bushes. It's in the details, of course, and I'm only giving a skeletal view. But it's the comic that drives me. The "tragic" has more orderly existence, even in its trajectory; only the "comic" can make sense (or non-sense) of our *disordered* universe where all of us are just hanging on. I'd have to spell out all the details, in each of the narratives, to explain or clarify, but I'm not in the mood for that kind of personalism. I will sit you down sometime, gorgeous reader, and tell you everything—all the hesitations and masquerades—so you can understand. In the meantime, reread Melville's *The Confidence Man*, an American epic, or just turn to smoke and remake yourself.

The paradigm of all this occurred when I was fifteen and living in one of five identical three-story, twelve-unit buildings in a heavily Jewish neighborhood—in Pittsburgh. My high school, Taylor Allderdice, was the scene of violence almost every afternoon at 3:05 when school was let out. Like Gaul, the building was divided into three parts—and a different group came out of and entered each of the three doors. The one on the north was where the upper-middle-class Wasps left in their cars. The one in the middle was for the Jews, mostly lower middle class, children of salesmen, small-store owners, craftsmen, starving lawyers, and dentists. The southern entrance the Hunkies used, sons and daughters of millworkers, most of whom left school early in their lives to go to work where their fathers did, or in the case of girls, to find a suitable husband. "Hunkies" was the pejorative term for the mass of Eastern Europeans working for U.S. Steel, Alcoa, Westinghouse, and the like, excluding I guess, blacks, who were certainly not Hunkies but perhaps Italians who were dragged in with the other fish. The word in Cleveland was "Bohunks." James Laughlin, founder of New Directions, the famous publishing company and heir to Jones and Laughlin Steel, J&L, told me that at the dinner table it was one of the joys to tell jokes about, or belittle, women, blacks, Jews, and Hunkies. It was their amusement. He hated his family and their friends. The Hunkies, who felt mistreated, underpaid, unacknowledged, overseen, blamed the Jews (of the middle entrance) for their abuses and insulted and beat up particularly the smaller isolated Jewish boys, especially those with glasses—and books—and one time so hurt one of them that he suffered permanent brain damage, from sticks, kicks, punches, whatnot. The school authorities did little—maybe nothing—about it. They didn't explain, or didn't know even, the class structure, anti-Semitism, conversion (or sublimation) of wrongs, the innocence of Jews, who had absolutely nothing to do with steel mills which they neither owned nor worked in, at any level. Certainly the Croatians, Hungarians, Polish, Russians, and Romanians brought their hatred of Jews over on the boats with them. Certainly their children were merely repeating what they heard at home and, as often as not, in church. I was fifteen, a sophomore in high school, and outraged. So were my friends. I had very little advanced understanding, in my middle door, than the wilder and angrier ones had in the lower, south, door.

To call anti-Semitism a (social) aberration of the 1930s and '40s is unequivocally incorrect. It is a widespread pathology, an affliction, that has existed for centuries, and not only in Europe and the Americas but worldwide. I experienced it constantly, directly and indirectly, physically, violently. Not only have Jews been herded into barns and the barns set on fire—in Eastern Europe—and years after the Holocaust, but they have been persecuted in a dozen ways, in Romania, Hungary, Pennsylvania, Michigan, Georgia, Alabama, Argentina. Only the existence—and madness—of racism, white hatred of blacks has partially obscured it. And it exists today even in communities where there are very few Jews, or none. A very close friend of mine from Texas told me about a twelve-year-old girl held down by some older boys and the word "Jew" was written on her neck with a magic marker. This in 2016. She apparently was too frightened—or ashamed—to tell her teacher. I don't know how it was that much different from German soldiers in the late 1930s, forcing bearded Jews to clean sidewalks with toothbrushes, in Berlin or some other hellhole.

In my little world, spokesperson that I always was, I found myself a kind of leader. I proposed that we cut up one-inch garden hose, liberally supplied in the basements, and partially melt some of the lead piled up in the backyards—for building—and stuff pieces in both ends of one-foot rubber lengths, thus creating lissome blackjacks. We organized, literally, a small army, twenty, thirty, forty of us, and surrounded the southernmost exit about ten minutes before the bell sounded for the end of the school day. We all left our classes early, and when our enemies came out we clubbed them with the blackjacks, probably hurting some of them badly, and thus—in five minutes—ended the assault on Jews. As I write about it now, it does seem extreme and murderous and I am a little horrified.

The police did come (finally) and we were carted down in Black Marias to juvenile court, where I spent my first night in custody. I made a long speech to the magistrate explaining and justifying our actions, and I was identified as a leader and troublemaker. We were released the next morning, probably with a warning, but for the next two years that I was at that school, there were two or three policemen patrolling the area, especially in the afternoon when school was dismissed. We worked at one of the long tables—I remember—in one of the basements, cutting the hoses with our sharpened jackknives and forcing the chunks of lead into either end. We had a little factory and finished our work in no time. Always given to singing, I led a Volga work-shanty, which made our work both exotic and unreal. For me, it was joyous. I always loved work. It was also comic—that was the key—and we made a huge joke of the whole matter, anticipating the event, the engagement to come, and congratulating ourselves on our great plans. There was a serious side and a ridiculous side to it. It was also "edgy," as we would say now, and risk-taking, and it set the pattern for the other similar events that would occur—for me—in the next few decades. I don't talk about these things with pride, though there still is a certain self-aggrandizement—or congratulatory impulse—to the thing. I am more ashamed—embarrassed is the word—at my attitude, the distance, the secrecy, finally the complacency and comfort. Nor am I unaware how modest and how "local" the protests and actions were. I should have wasted my energy—*if* I was compelled to spend it—on a bigger stage. I am rehashing it now only for one reason: to finally get rid of it altogether, to bury it or burn it, so I'll never have to refer to it in any way again forever. And I only respond to individual acts of injustice now—in addition to my roaring—by singing or by listening to music or watching old movies. God knows that I'm sick of ranting—by the left or the right. Though I don't mean to say that I have turned against witnessing and protest; and I loved the anarchy on Wall Street, a year or so ago; and I couldn't stand Bloomberg's stupid response.

My mind goes back to Tuli Kupferberg and the Fugs. My son, David, and I listened to his "River of Shit" in the 1970s, along with Mississippi John Hurt. Steel is gone and the Hunkies moved—with everyone else—to the suburbs, got college degrees, and studied art as well as accounting. The ones who went to Allderdice lived in Greenfield, Warhola lived in Lower Greenfield with the Carpatho-Russians. Jews no long killed Christ or drank Christian blood. Pope John praised them for their *faith*. That which they were once murdered for. My guess is there were about a million killed by the bloodthirsty Europeans, since 1000 CE. I am not counting those humiliated, jailed, tortured, and ghettoized, and I carry in my body the memory of insults—and punches—that came my way. I had to become a type of warrior to combat it. Though the worst were the "insults from on high," a combination of ignorance and arrogance. This was America from "Irish need not apply" to the Chinese Exclusion Act. I don't know which came first. A Jew was in jeopardy, in my day, if he applied for work in a large corporation, say Mellon Bank or U.S. Steel. He—she—was subject to quotas at the university. He had to have a perfect grade average—plus political pull—to get into medical school. He—she—knew where *not* to apply. He was good at getting messages and knew when to stay away. If this is true for Jews it's true for blacks to the nth degree. God, I knew what discomfort was! If it doesn't exist today like that, that's beside the point. Once it exists it always exists. Nothing disappears. And I'll carry it to the grave with me. And I guess that's what this book is about, assuming it's a book, the things you carry to the grave with you. And I mean it most literally, as well as metaphorically. Just think of me all alone down there. I'm almost thinking of what I'll take with me—the pens and paper, the books, the coffee, the nice bread I buy at the all-night market on Broadway and 110th when it's just baked and have the butcher put it in his slicing machine and wrap it in plastic and slap a price on its side. And a light, a light that never goes out.

In the industrial towns along the three rivers, only the old and the very old are left, the children and grandchildren have moved to the suburbs and have taken up white-collar trades, accounting, teaching, computers, managers, real estate, most of which requires college training. I don't know if there's much intermarriage (I know of some), but I doubt if Jews are blamed for *all* the miseries. I only go back to Pittsburgh to give readings and talks, never to look up relatives, of which there are certainly a few left. I now consider myself part Hunkie—I am even going to apply for Polish citizenship. I'm deeply sorry about the blackjacks. And I have no enemies in either Upper or Lower Greenfield.

My Sullen Art

Bolaño said, in *Savage Detectives*, that what started as comedy ends as tragedy. He also said it ends as tragicomedy. He also said it ends, inevitably, as comedy. He also said a cryptographic exercise, a horror movie, a triumphal march, a mystery, a dirge in the void, and a comic monologue. Tragic is easier to describe, though pathos and the maudlin get in the way. Aristotle can't be beat. I got a call yesterday from a friend in Iowa, which reminds me that the University of Iowa Press is bringing out a collection of my drawings and cartoons, which gives some idea of what the comic is to me, at least the graphic comic. I was given to realistic drawings beginning when I was six or seven and to cartoons from the time I was nineteen or twenty. I recall that the best of them had a seriocomic nature (I almost said "thrust"), and I wished they hadn't disappeared. Furthermore, they had a mysterious and insane lucidity about them—I am talking about my very

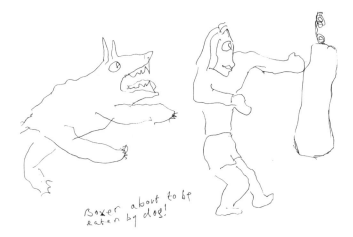

Boxer about to be
eaten by dog!

old cartoons—that defied even me to understand them or
be able to explain them. The most recent ones are mostly
plays on words, puns and such, most of them quickly rec-
ognizable. I've reproduced one above and on page 140 is
one I drew last night that reminded me of the earlier one.

It is this one I am most interested in now, and whose
comic nature I want most to understand and—if possible—explain. I see that it didn't need any writing and
would, in addition, operate on—or in—a different level
or place. It might penetrate deeper were the writing ex-
cluded, plus it might *include* the explanation anyhow. But
without the explanation there may be more of the "insane

lucidity" I spoke about, or perhaps not—perhaps it needed the words to create that. I would also like to remark that the artist's (the cartoonist's) seriousness and head-on devotion helps create the "crazy" humor, as in Kafka, if I can say so. It's also the devil-may-care quick take that adds to the comic. Also the roughness and inartistic nature of the renderings. The very bafflement is a part of the comic, as well as the fact that the two figures are each obsessed with different objects, or purposes, the boxer with hitting the heavy bag, the dog with attacking (eating) the boxer. They are part of my imagination, perhaps part of my experience—so to speak. The fact that the figures are more or less outlines, that they (both of them now, I see) are faced in the same direction, and intent on their activity helps create the comic, as well as that the eye of the dog and the eye of the boxer are more or less identical. My favorite parts are the left foot of the boxer and the (anatomically incorrect) left foot of the dog. I love the dog's ferocity and the boxer's innocence. The dog has the teeth, the boxer is more or less unmuscled. Sometimes what I am *attempting* to achieve can be captured in a movie, on rare occasions in a self-portrait. Still, the viewer has to get it without the criticism or the explanation. It may be something else to him or her, or neither.

I'm not sure if the "comic" of my cartoons comes from the same place as that in my writing. The play on words belongs a little too much to "entertainment." The boxer comes from that place, and others like it, I guess. It's the humanity, when that exists, that is the commonality. The implication of suffering, and kindness, the human condition understood as walking on ice, hanging on with two fingers, your pants not going on over your boots, and someone knocking. Your sister with a fiend. Bush stealing the presidency, Humphrey being loyal once too often, the pedals broken on your bicycle again, a window broken and

the air coming in, a thief smoking a cigarette on your dol-
lar, your roof leaking, a dead squirrel in your rain barrel,
a police car's lights, a foot of water in your cellar, a lost
bat, a false beginning to your poem, a false beginning to
your story, a letter in the mail, a "dead" opossum in your
garbage can, dog shit in your garbage can, a painful back,
a lost notebook, your battery dead; but, on the other hand,
a hefty check to surprise you, a good friend calling you
up, your computer working, your radio, your phone, your
Hoover, working. Is there more bad than good? The comic
is a way of handling loss, one way; and a way of explaining
the inexplicable.

When I was twenty-two, unemployed and thread-
bare, my friends at City Hall (Pittsburgh)—or the county
courthouse—heard of a job on the books that had never
actually been filled; it was called the Librarian of the
Commonwealth, and there was no job description whatsoever, and the salary would be arranged in Harrisburg,
the state capital, between you and the "broker." It was part
of a spoils system that you did absolutely nothing to earn,
and based exclusively on friendship, with no strings attached. All I had to do was get a sheet of paper notarized
that would attest to my party loyalty (Democrat) and my
education (BA). Which I did at an alderman's office, he

a party hack, a slightly famous name and the father of a boyhood chum of mine, whose house I had been to often. It was a done deal. The next week—as directed—I went to Harrisburg to meet with the appointed person, a state senator. In the meantime I spent hours thinking of what my uniform would be and what kind of job I would carve out for myself. But when I arrived for the meeting, I was informed—by the state senator—that a different wing of the party had just taken over and the job was no longer his to give. Thus my position as Librarian of the Commonwealth suddenly turned to smoke and I was once more eating dried lima beans and ketchup. I don't think that anyone else got the job. I don't know what happened. That's a sad story, isn't it? Part of that "human condition" I referred to. But you should have seen me in my getup, boots, jacket, etc., and the office I never occupied, and the good works I never did, and the title I never had. Though I suffered very little from it, I was so busy with other dreams.

Now I'm done with "acts" and I'm done talking about it. For a small time I abandoned the political for the aesthetic, a good 1950s position, but I soon found a way of combining the two, with neither being a servant. I tread lightly, even humorously on some things that were of deep importance to me and even have remained so in retrospect. But I still go crazy over little things that others might just not notice. Some things are comic from the start, and some things are "comic" in a broad and philosophical way—but are not "funny." That—the funny—I rather abhor. I will be eighty-nine in a few weeks. Our expectations, in regard to age, are relative and cultural. I don't sit, a sage, in a seat of honor combing my white beard with my manicured nails, with my grandchildren, even my great-grandchildren, one at a time coming to sit on my lap and be hugged, then kissed, as a type of blessing, all of sixty-eight or even seventy, an ancient and revered age. I could be the (young) father of such a person. Nor do I have a beard, let alone a white one; and my nails are neither long nor manicured. My grandchildren are scattered, in Wellesley, Massachusetts, and Huntsville, Alabama. The youngest is going on four, the oldest is fourteen. Their Zadee should be twenty years younger than he is. And to my sadness, years could pass between my seeing them, and many months before even talking to them. But forget the chair, the blessing, and such bullshit. I am reading Trinity University Press's *Mexican Writers on Writing*, edited by Margaret Sayers Peden. A terrific book. I'm particularly interested in the youngest of the writers presented, those born in the late

1940s and early 1950s, what they're doing and how they're being received. In 1948, when the Mexican Army was invading universities and killing students, I was in my early forties, wandering through New York, now the Lower East, now the Upper West. My new voice had come to me a few years earlier, and I was absolutely sure of what I was doing and where I was going. I was getting some recognition, that absurd gift. Even in subways and at bus stops. At one bus stop a coming program of a performance by a string quartet was pasted inside the glass enclosure with a poem of mine praising the harpsichordist, a friend of mine, Elaine Comparone, who accompanied the quartet. The poem was called "Elaine Comparone," and I was tempted to point out its beauty to the others waiting there, sitting glumly or checking their watches. The Mexican book gives me the names of the writers—mostly novelists, now in their sixties, over ten years older than I was then, practicing, as I did, my "sullen art."

A Year's Diary

Last winter, in Florida, I decided to keep a diary for exactly one year, but starting on my birthday, February 22 (2013), which I kept up till almost the end of September (2013), or a total of seven months and a few days. I had a notebook dedicated to it, and now I'm reading the notebook, the diary. I can say that the beginning was more interesting than the ending, the entries longer, the subjects, in the beginning, diverse as well as lengthy, the end sheer notation or reporting of facts. I'm going to reproduce the first two entries and the last three.

Here are the first two:

February 22

> I don't know what use a year's diary is to me or to the world, nor do I know that other writers are doing this but I am determined to keep a diary this time, not of the year 2013 but of my own year, starting today on my

birthday, February 22nd, and ending on February 21st, 2014, since I have no doubt—at least this morning—I will live it out.

Anne Marie plans for us to go this evening to dinner at the Provence, on Lincoln Road (we are spending a month in Miami Beach, from February 1st to the 28th in a huge depressing building, or series of buildings—at 15th and the Bay, just above West Avenue, a block east of Alton Road and maybe twelve blocks west of the famous noisy strip by the ocean called South Beach). It turns out my mother and father lived at 11th and West, four blocks from here, till he died, in 1969, and she till her death in 1993, twenty-seven years in her case. It looks different now than it did then—the small cottages by the bay are gone and there are only—or mostly—very large apartment houses, restaurants, banks, and other businesses. Where she lived was called Forte Towers, named for the builder. I used to visit her twice a year, doing her taxes, holding her hand, defending myself from her bossiness, happy to go back to the snow.

We ate with Chase Twitchell, a fine poet, raised in Connecticut. She brought me a present, a light-responsive plastic doll—Queen Elizabeth—who would wave her right arm when we put her near the candle. I

have known Chase for years, along with her husband,
Russell Banks. They spend six months (and a day) in
Miami Beach and the rest of the time at their place in
the Adirondacks. We ended up telling jokes, WASP
and Jewish. The longer I live the more I realize how
significant culture is. Jews and WASPs now marry each
other, but their worlds are utterly different. She talked
about her mother; I would get along with her because of
my elastic nature—but I wouldn't tell her any jokes—she
would be lost.

February 23

I remember last night Chase Twitchell talked a bit about
her times at the University of Alabama in Tuscaloosa.
I missed her by a couple of years, since I had the Coal
Chair there in—I think—1984, and she came later. She
knows that Jack Gilbert was a friend of mine and talked
about him when he was in residence (also the Coal
Chair, in 1986 I think). She drove him around, to grocery
stores and such. She recalls she drove him to one store
but he said the foodstuff was too dear, and he wanted to
shop where the poor people did. There he bought tuna
fish, and soup in dented cans, other cheap food. Anne
Marie says "All roads lead to Jack" and doesn't like me

talking about him, so I said very little. But there was my
old friend—dead of Alzheimer's this past November—
lecturing on love, dismissing the students, superior
as usual. Chase told me what I've known for sixty-five
years, that Jack couldn't swim, ride a bike, drive a car. I
didn't tell her about our aborted trip—in a 1935 Nash—to
Mexico. We both agreed he was a very special poet.
Anne Marie and Chase are meeting maybe every few
days to do yoga, eat lunch, and exchange poems. I am not
allowed to come.

I don't know who will read this stuff, someone who
wants to make a point maybe about my poetry. I would
enjoy, if that's the word—reading Céline's diary, Henry
Miller's, Cummings's—if they could be honest and open.
Maybe the diary will take over as a major art form.
Why not? We already have True Confessions to the 10th
power. Everybody laying himself—herself—bare. Last
night, when Anne Marie and I were returning to our
apartment, she nudged me and turning to my left there
was a woman dragging a suitcase after her, her hair wild,
a kind of very flimsy diaphanous robe on her shoulders,
and her body, large and sexy, clothed only in tight
underpants and a light bra, her buns round and inviting.
She meant it probably as "honest and open," as much as

provocative. But I'd hate to have to read what she would say in *her* diary. I find I can't record what happened to me without talking to someone, and I feel that that's maybe too "literary" for this form. But that's what I have to do. I must say that I'm just finishing the re- or re-rereading of *Jane Eyre*, and I can't resist the contrast between that wise, humble, and sweet creature and the woman in the see-through outfit. Jane would of course be shocked, as I was.

It's always a question of why people keep diaries. Letters we can understand—you're talking to someone. But who are you talking to in a diary, literary mankind? What is its history? Did Ovid keep a diary? Did Augustine? For that matter, did Alexander? Or Jesus? Charlemagne didn't, because he couldn't read or write. He could dictate though, couldn't he? To a scribe, a poet—who might take liberties? And what's the purpose of diaries? Or what force propels them? Wouldn't you love to read Nero's diaries? Or J. Edgar's? I would say, without consulting the Internet, that it's writers, and other artists of one kind or another, who mostly keep diaries, and government people, presidents, kings, diplomats, and such. I would also say that they're not—like novels—something you take to an agent, something for general consumption. They are more private, more personal, for your great-grandchildren, or for historians, or maybe for biographers. I remember Pepy's and Evelyn's diaries of the late seventeenth century from my early reading. They were published early in the nineteenth century and, as far as England was concerned, were the first to move the diary from business concerns to personal experience, as in ancient Egyptian notations on papyrus concerning business matters moved (later) into histories of the pharaohs and then into religion and poetry.

Marcus Aurelius wrote a kind of diary called "To Myself" that must anticipate the dozens and dozens of diaries written by other emperors—and their minions. Particularly the modern ones in Russia, France, Spain, Italy, and the United States. Japanese court ladies wrote pillow books, and there were diaries written in Arabic as early as the tenth century. There were also diaries written by medieval mystics concerned with the personal as spiritual, and they were popular in Florence and Venice during the Renaissance. The three most popular kinds seem to have been love, travel, and political diaries. Some were eventually published, some were lost or destroyed.

There is the diary of Anne Frank, edited by her father; Carl Jung's diary; Anaïs Nin's and Robert Musil's and Edmund Wilson's. My grandfather, Beryl Barach, kept a diary—also for one year (a calendar year: 1911)—written in a language of his own that combined Yiddish and Hebrew, which I own but have not yet gotten translated. I believe it contains pious truisms and not shocking revelations, that remote chicken-killer and Malamud. I believe the reason I got bored with my own diary is not only that I'm not disciplined but that I've "told it all," in my poetry, my essays, and my interviews. I could have used the occasion to construct a "last testament," as in "Last Will and Testament," but I don't really have anything new to say. I do have a will and it does say in the very first sentence "Last Will and Testament," but it's all about money and property and not testimonial. That is a thing of the past. Though I realize I do have a short testament, in *Stealing History*, the book I published in 2012.

So I'm doing a testament after all. My will is simple and I instruct my children, my grandchildren, and three "stepchildren" to read pages 172–173 from *Stealing History*. I am reprinting it here for the hungry readers' elucidation. May my readers be blessed (for reading me), may they keep a diary, tell the truth, lie, blaspheme, get on their knees, stand on their heads, hold their breath, do nine one-handed push-ups, swim for hours, climb steps, stand in awe of two things, stop texting, eat goose eggs, visit Bessarabia, love snow, and never call a coffin a casket.

> I believe human beings should pay very close attention to each other. They should reach out beyond the family and help the oppressed, the trapped, and the sick. They should insist on security for and from the larger society. They should pay attention to the past, live with grief, make charity personal, teach without end, share food, listen patiently to the young and honor their music, turn their backs on corporations, advertising, and public lying, hate liars, undermine bullies, love June 21, and, on that day, kiss every plant and tree they see. They should love two-lane highways, old cars and old songs. They should eat with relish, and study insects. They should never stop raising children. They should fight for schoolteachers, *pay them*, give them tenure, let *them* make the rules. As Coca-Cola does. They should insist that no one be paid more than ten times anyone else, no matter what or where. They should make fun of war, flags, uniforms, weapons, pulpits, oval offices,

square ones, oblong ones, circular ones; and robes, and
titles, especially the titles of "Dr." given to education
degree holders in state colleges who address each other
as "Doctor." They should respect all dogs, love one
breed intensely, eat fruit, eat root vegetables, read *Lear*
endlessly, and be suspicious of Gertrude Stein—with the
exception of her war plays. They should love New York,
know two foreign languages, practice both regret and
remorse, love their own cities, forgive but not forget,
live in at least three countries, work in a gas station,
lift boxes, eat pears, learn a trade, respect pitch pines,
believe in the soul. They should stop throwing rubbish
out the window, they should sit on park benches, marry
young, marry late, love seals, love cows, talk to apes,
weep for tigrons, cheer on the carp, encourage the
salmon and the shad, and read twenty books a year. They
should talk to their neighbors and eat herring and boiled
potatoes.

And here are the last three diary entries:

Sunday September 22

Stockton Market. Food for lunch—at my house. No
Everett—says he'll be here Monday.

Monday September 23

Steph here all day—Ross for lunch. Prose brought up to date. Called Everett—late. Said he'll be here on Tuesday.

Tuesday September 24

Everett showed up at 9:15.

New Year's Party

I am one of those who tend to like the countdown to the new year and even—when the occasion arises—join vociferously the public counting, not so much as if we're accounting the ten seconds before the new year begins but as if we were referees counting the old year out, the Joe Palooka, the Primo Carnera, year of cauliflower ears and split swollen lips, and readying ourselves to hold up the arm of the new champion, barely tested, breathing evenly, a smile on his golden face, the ball dropping, the world kissing, and everyone determined to start from scratch and do it right this time. So reminiscent of my mother turning the brilliant ceiling light on on Saturday night and wishing everyone within earshot *"A gute voch"* as we started the new week supposedly full of hope, though her voice was tremulous and, as often as not, one of the bulbs was out, spreading an unwelcome darkness throughout the room. Though I respect and even grudgingly admire the cynics, those miserable dogs, who announce with great confidence that it's just like any other night—and they prefer not to put their formal wear on, and that they'll probably go to bed at 10:30 or 11:00, and the last thing they want is to stare at a stupid image of folks in Times Square drunk with joy or those in Chicago, Denver, and Seattle still waiting, an hour or two or three away from the drunken moment.

A Walpurgis Nacht of sorts, though that is the holiday that—formally—brings in spring even if not by the calendar, the first of May, celebrated for ten different reasons. International Labor Day, which began, as we saw, in Chicago; moving day (in Pittsburgh); the setting of bonfires (and unrestrained sexual activity) in Germany, Sweden, Norway, and the Baltics, simultaneously identified as the end of the school year—in those countries; and the liberation of the students, large picnics, playing of music, dancing, akin to the hopelessly moderate maypole activities in such places as Smith and Wellesley; a mystical time, the witches misbehaving on the hills and in the forests, the wildness taking over. A little different from the ball dropping in Times Square and kissing—mostly with unopened mouth—your beloved. Too bad the wildness never truly took over on New Year's Eve. Maybe it was too cold. It's hard to have a picnic, or cavort, when it's five below.

It may not have been that cold, though it was freezing, when a few friends came up to our apartment on 110th Street. Anne Marie, not only a profoundly gifted and original poet but a caretaker of her aging parents and her—equally aging—and somewhat cantankerous common-law husband, a term we both prefer to "partner," her C.L.H., namely Yaakov, whose American name is the much-preferred (by some) "Gerald," which I certainly said elsewhere means spear-wielder in Old German, made a beautiful dinner, risotto with mushrooms, roast chicken, salad, brussels sprouts, pie and ice cream. We were all writers there. One of us, Kristoff Keller, married to the poet and biographer Jan Heller Levi, is confined to a wheelchair because of a progressive nerve disease, and we had a complicated time bringing him up the three outside steps since the building had apparently disposed of its ramp. Although I was repeatedly promised there'd be one and we ended up carrying him in in the wheelchair. The doorman was unbelievably rude and obtuse, even insulting, and at one point suggested that Jan and Kristoff should go back home when we refused his offer of a quarter-inch plywood for a makeshift ramp. Kristoff, a Swiss-German who writes beautifully in both German and English, to be humiliated this way. Harold Schechter, one of the husbands, brought to me as a gift four books on dying, death, and undertakers to help me with my prose since I'd already told him how useful his own book on death and dying was. Harold is a specialist on serial murders and horror films but is a very lovely, gentle, and deeply intelligent man.

We spent a happy evening together in spite of the doorman, even though there weren't any bonfires, may-poles, or leftist speeches. I guess everyone there knew there wouldn't ever—at least in our time—be a general strike, though I am certain everyone there regretted the conversion of May Day into Labor Day, the time of bringing in the boats and starting the fall semester, those of us who were teaching or had children still at schools. I suspect I may have been the only one who remembered the fall semester starting long after the first frost, and associated it with wool sports jackets and even flannel shirts, with or without neckties. We have been cheated of many things at our colleges the last sixty years, but the one thing that even the classicists among us hardly ever mentions is the joy of kicking leaves as we carry a clean copy of the *Aeneid* under our right arm and an uncut Latin dictionary, looking for the nearest table to begin once again, the Sybil, Dido, everything over again, only this time for good.

Harold's books—the ones he gave me—included a novel by Jim Crace called *Being Dead*, the story of a double murder (husband and wife), two zoologists who were killed in the dunes by a drifter, where he, the husband, had first slept with his wife shortly after they first met, as biology students doing investigations and research—at this beach, a group of them, staying at a nearby house, which burned to the ground while they were there. Her project had been the study of the oceanic bladder fly, and his was the study of the spray hopper who survived, who flourished, in the waves. He was bringing his wife back to the scene of her seduction god knows how many years ago, but they discovered that a large number of new houses were being built there and it was even difficult to get to the beach itself and once again find a hospitable dune. Though she, who caught his drift, was reluctant, if submissive. Two professors returning to the scene of the crime, with absolutely no thought of what lay in store for them. The murderer was in search of anything he could either use or sell, phones, cameras, cash, jewelry, watches, binoculars, cigarettes, some food, clothes. He was heartless and had no feelings for the two people he killed. He struck them with a rock, a piece of granite that fit perfectly in his hand, her first, then him—and left them there—in the dunes, unclothed, just as they were—except with their heads split open. The rest of the novel, told in alternating threads or narratives, deals with their lives together, their jobs, their one daughter and the search for them once it was realized they were missing—with meetings pending and the like. Though they were a bloody mess when they finally were discovered—in their underclothes, dead, his hand holding on to her ankle. What interests me is the precise, and exhausting, knowledge Crace has about the bodies after they've died—the stages (again) of their decomposition. It's almost as if his real interest was biological decay. In fact I felt, while reading the book, that Crace had to be a student of biology—or a mortician—before he became a novelist, he knew so much. But novelists do read books.

A beetle, he says, was the first to discover the bodies. Then came the swag flies and the crabs, summoned by the fresh wounds and the smell of urine. Then a gull who both feasted on the crabs and nibbled at the loose flesh of the dead zoologists. Crace waxes poetic on the beetle: "He didn't carry with him any of that burden which makes the human animal so cumbersome, the certainty that death was fast approaching and could arrive at any time, with its plunging snout," and "He had not spent, like us, his lifetime concocting systems to deny mortality or had he passed his days in melancholic fear of death. He had no schemes, no memories, no guilt or aspirations, no appetite for love, no delusions."

The book abounded with this kind of information. There was no "meaning" in death, unless it was what could be called "meaningless." He almost enjoys the descriptions of the deteriorating bodies. Pallid on the upper parts, livid on the undersides. He, dead on his back, was "white-faced and purple-shouldered. His lips, though, were drawn and blue, his gums had shrunk . . . His nose had sunk into his face." Finally the swag fly maggots and the dismantling. Crace's message, for there is a message, is simple and I would say disappointing in its banality. "There is no future and no past. There is no remedy for death—or birth—except to hug the spaces in between. Live loud. Live wide. Live tall." A little more boring than "they are already in Paradise." An excellent novel, but for its pep song.

We were eating our pie and talking away at each other, eight of us, though I was a little quieter than I usually am. I was thinking of some other New Year's Eve dinners, or parties, one a sexual (feast) in Philadelphia where, I remember, there was just fucking and nothing to eat or drink, not even a cracker or a cup of Cribari Brothers; one in Indiana, Pennsylvania, where we ate a late supper—the style in (German) Pennsylvania—and I tasted pork cooked in sauerkraut for the very first time in my life; and one in Glasgow, where the holiday is called Hogmanay and you go from house to house with a lump of coal as a gift, or a blessing. I ended up there sitting on the floor against a wall with a Scottish poet named Willie, I called him Wee Willie, the two of us singing a dumb but haunting song all our time there as a kind of background to the general merriment, a very sad song. Wee Willie died six months later from tuberculosis, a killer in Glasgow in those days. I loved Willie and—despite Crace, if I could mix the time and alternate realities—I mourned him, a very thin, a very dear poet, who didn't own an overcoat.

I was also, even while talking, thinking of the four books Harold gave me and anxious to get to them as early in 2014 as I could, certainly before breakfast on January first, the next day. I was thinking that you could concentrate at least on three things at once, in my case the subject at hand, the nominal subject; second, the methodology of thinking or thinking of thinking itself; and, third, the underlying subject, in my case death itself, at least, in my case, my dying, my burial, and, naturally, the concomitant thinking through my own life and, naturally, the book I am more or less fitfully writing, which I think is fine, only on two tracks. Though I have discovered that when you think of as many as five things at a time you tend to lose one or two of them either from time to time or permanently. I don't know how many tracks the others at the table had but, even if they were multiple, they had to be different and, in most cases, different from me, or from mine.

I didn't get to all of the books for several weeks and, in one case, for months. They were buried deep in the trunk of Anne Marie's car and would appear, from time to time, almost always *on time* when I was ready for them. Now that the flowers have arrived, after a long and surprisingly bitter winter, I'm having pleasant and playful thoughts again about the afterlife, though I tend here to agree with Crace that everything was born to die, even us, and that's it. "The earth," he says, "is practiced in the craft of burial." But I don't take any pleasure from it; I grieve for it, though I'm not—not now—going to weep for it, I have other things to weep for besides this.

There was very little boisterousness that night and no singing. No guitars or mouth organs. Not even a bad joke. We all went down together to the lobby, and those of us who could carried the wheelchair outside. The *occupied* wheelchair. We hugged and kissed and said goodbye in the cold. Up here—on the Upper West Side—there is always a wind blowing. Sometimes it's small and sometimes it has a good deal of force. I remember it being halfway between one and the other and that it was a relief to re-enter the lobby and take the elevator to the fourth floor. It was a lot earlier than other New Year's were, but you get civilized—read restrained—as the years catch up with you. As quiet takes over and we leave the pots and pans till the next day. A civilized thing to do.

Truth is, while we were eating our pie I was thinking of what death had in store for me, and I was particularly thinking of the biblical three score and ten and how practically another score has passed since that year. I do remember my seventieth birthday, with my son and daughter-in-law in Boston, and my daughter's wedding in Tucson a short time after that, me in a cheap tuxedo and a useless right arm, the result of a truck colliding with me during a sudden snowstorm on I-95 on the way into Philadelphia, and how my car skidded to a stop, an inch or so from a huge ditch or an abyss, which might have caused a little more trouble than a stiff arm, which I walked and swam my way out of.

On my eightieth Anne Marie organized a huge celebration at a marvelous restaurant in Lambertville. I
think we took over most of the tables and ate and drank
sans cesse. I remember Dylan, my grandson from David
and Diane, was a baby then, crawling on the floor. He is
now in his ninth year, readying himself to be a professional basketball player. Nothing suddenly happened to
me that night by way of health or radical change in one
way or other; for that matter nothing happened in the
decade (almost) that followed except for a deterioration
in my back muscles or a problem with my nerve endings
that causes me to be much slower and to use a cane. This
is hard for me for I have been so mobile in my life and
have walked endlessly—even great distances. Swimming
is fine but the nearest pool is an hour away. I don't know
if—at this time—more people die in their seventies or
eighties, but I'm sure that fewer make it into their nine-
ties. Occasionally someone reaches a hundred, and in odd
places like the Crimea, they last sometimes till the 110th
or even 120th, which is attributed to the large quantity
of cucumbers they eat (with yogurt on top) or how they
stare at trees. My generation of poets has been decimated.
Many have died; some have dementia. I think there are
six of us left—or four. From the time you're sixty-five (or

seventy), when asked about your "state" you tend to say, "I'm thankful I got up this morning." I have to say I never stooped that low. If you're "healthy," you get in the habit of *living* day after day after week after month. And you only think of your own passing when you visit a doctor, or your vision is blurred, or there is an odd lump on your body, or a giving up of blood.

The main thing to know is that death, at least in the elderly, is not the invasion or accident that it, finally, seems to be but a natural, an inevitable, phenomenon. And if "the cause" of death must be cancer, Alzheimer's, stroke, or heart attack, it must be said that in old age, the defenses break down so that the real cause of death in elders is just "old age." For in old age the cells weaken, the circulation is slowed by the buildup of plaque and the narrowing of the arteries, the death of cardiac muscle, disorderly heart rhythms, actual occlusion, swelling of tissue, edema, infections, inflammations, inadequate blood flow to the brain, kidney and liver failure, death of cells and failure of replenishment, stroke, decline of the immune system, blood poisoning, as well as malignancy and dementia. Among our elder eldest, I read, the risk of stroke is thirty times as great as it is for the younger, those still in their seventies. Does this mean that deep respect among the extended family has been converted to terror? I'm remembering a line of my own poetry now: "I was always the youngest." What should I have done otherwise than what I did? Shouldn't there be a chapter—in the books of wisdom—called "elder happiness"? Am I suffering from that? We didn't dance that night—none of us danced. When I was twenty I went crazy dancing the polka. I know I dance with part of my tongue sticking out, as if I'm going to bite the end of it off. "How can I, that girl standing there, / my attention fix . . . / ah, dancer, ah, sweet dancer . . ." Montaigne died at fifty-nine; Shakespeare, fifty-six; Picasso, ninety-two; Eddy Cantor, seventy-two; Bartók, sixty-five. Dear Bob Summers, dear Larry Levis, dear Sylvia.

Nina Cassian

Nina Cassian died—suddenly—in her apartment on Roosevelt Island in New York City. I don't know if there were any warnings in the days leading up to the incident, but she was either waterlogged or her passageways had narrowed—and hardened—or closed up altogether. The *Times* called it a heart attack. Nina, who was a few months older than me, was one of the leading Romanian poets of the past hundred years. She was in America—in the late 1980s—when some of her letters to a friend in Bucharest were seized by the Romanian secret police, thus compromising her and making her return to Romania extremely dangerous. She asked for, and received, asylum in the U.S. I met her in Iowa City where she was in residence with the International Writing Program—the IWP. We became friends, read each other's poems, and traveled to New York together at the end of her stay in Iowa. I found her to be brilliant, gifted—and difficult. She was a feminist but adored—and expected—the traditional male courtesies. Which I tend not to be a practitioner of—such things, for example, as carrying all the suitcases and searching for them when they are lost in airports. She proposed to me; if I married her, she said, we would move to an island in the Black Sea and all I'd have to do is "write my beautiful poems."

I went with her and a few others to a Romanian restaurant and dance hall in Queens, and when the orchestra realized she was there they came to our table and played on their knees before her. Later still, she came to my NYU apartment where I was having a Sunday gathering and, arriving early, she turned down some wine and rather formally announced that, as soon as her memoir was done she would be finished with this life and—almost in the same breath—asked me if I had any wodka, which I did, in the freezer. She was romantic, melancholy, harsh, respectful, and reverential. She was of the best our century had to offer. I understood that she used a walker at the end and complained a little. I am sorry we lost touch. She was a magnificent poet and a dear soul, born Renée Annie Katz. There is a special chair for her on that island in the Black Sea.

Dogs

When my mind is empty and I'm—sometimes—lying down and on the verge of drifting off, I remember the dogs in my life and how important they were to me. Though the fact is that, except for two weeks once, I never owned a dog. But I've written about them and I'm intrigued by the connections between humans and dogs—who adopted whom, maybe who civilized whom. I wrote a poem in Alabama once about a dead dog lying in a ditch at the side of the road uttering his last thoughts (though dead) as I am (maybe) uttering mine (though alive) in this crazy tract. Last testament for both of us. The poem was anthologized and I had to send in a photo of me and "my dog." Since I didn't have a dog I sent in a picture of me and a dog named Dolly, a spitz eskimo that belonged to a friend of mine living in Oxford, Iowa, Peter Feldstein. I love that affection seems to be the natural expression of dogs, maybe it's the natural expression of all mammals—though I don't think of insects, but who knows? Maybe it's not hunger or desire that divides us, but affection.

I may be wrong on this, but I think that more women than men seem to keep dogs, certainly women that live alone. Maybe they keep dogs so they can have someone, some thing to whom they can express their affection. Maybe it's women who are childless or whose children, or husbands, are gone. All too obvious. Peter (Feldstein) may be the one in his marriage who has the major needs. Though Josephine is certainly affectionate and loved Dolly. What they have now, years later, for pets I don't know. I do know that Peter is the classic "uncle," making faces and playing the clown. The clown children love. He of whom it is always said, "Too bad he didn't have children."

In my long life I've known many women with dogs. One left her husband and automatically took the dog with her. There was no question. Not that the husband didn't love the dog. The wife loved him more. One woman had a fat flatulent German shepherd who occupied the bottom of the staircase, forcing anyone who wanted to go upstairs, say to the bedroom, to climb over his body, a three-stair challenge. This woman, when she walked her dog, would either pull at his leash or shout "heel," the meaning of which I don't think he ever learned. It was the only dog I ever knew who positively—and specifically—disliked me, and I must say the feelings were mutual, for one thing, and that it wasn't difficult to transfer those emotions to the mistress, a willful, stubborn, selfish, cheap person.

One woman I knew had a dog that was a cross between a cocker spaniel and some kind of bird, a cockatoo, I think. I didn't dislike this dog, it just got on my nerves with its barking and because I was expected to share the walking duties, down and up five flights at the time and no elevator. I must admit he was a good dog who had the sense to be grateful. But even he had his mouth open and his tongue out when he reached the fourth floor. His mistress was a good person, but she wanted things from me I couldn't give her. That dog is long gone. So is another dog, who weighed maybe three pounds and was quiet and as unobtrusive as a stray leaf. She belonged to a woman with whom I spoke French who ended up teaching at a small college in Montreal. I liked them both. Louise Fishman, a former English student of mine at Tyler Art School, carried her little dog in her pocketbook when we went to a restaurant for lunch. She will have two gorgeous paintings in this year's Whitney Biennial. I love to sit on a bench in the little park at the foot of 111th Street and Riverside. I usually choose the one dedicated to Hyam and Rebecca

Gold, who loved to sit here in the early evening "reading, feeding birds, and admiring the passing dogs." So said their grandchildren who put up the small plaque. Dogs of all sorts come by, even the leashes are various. I met an imperial shih tzu yesterday, with a pug nose and very long brown and golden hair. His name is Oliver and he easily fits into his mistress's handbag. He was a service dog, she said, who, in this case, would call attention to her if she should have a diabetic seizure.

Andy

I am here for the third year in a row in Miami Beach, going
south like some of my winged cousins. We are in an apartment at First and Collins in what's called a penthouse and
consists, as far as the outdoors is concerned, of almost
the entire flat roof, fig trees, palms, three or four tables
and chairs, a kind of bar, lounge chairs, and a superb view
that lets us see the ocean a small block away, and six or so
forty-story buildings that occupy the extreme southern tip
of South Beach. Everywhere here it's glitz, money, elegant
cars, restaurants, and shops. A huge consumerville side
by side with a peaceful and half-empty beach. We have a
code to get into PH4 and a set of stairs with sixteen treads,
twelve and four (I'm still counting). On a large coffee table
in the small living room are several magazines in which
the city—almost desperately, and certainly despicably—
advertises itself. One of them advertises the (annual) art
show called Art Basel, held on Miami Beach, December

5–8, 2013. It's a peculiar magazine, presumably devoted to art, but featuring ads for eyeglasses, airlines, expensive automobiles, condos, estates, sweaters, watches, spas, hats; ridiculous serious models (male and female), shoes, leather jackets, food, kitchens, and bathrooms. One ad shows a naked young woman in very high heels talking into an old-timey phone from the roof of a building similar to ours. Her hair is short, blond, and unconvincingly windswept. Her pubic hair reaches very high up and is much darker. But it's not an ad! It seems to be part of a photographic portfolio put together by the curator at the International Center of Photography. The portfolio is not about the photos, it's about Miami.

> Miami is America's most exotic city. The allure of the pure white beaches, the brash sunlight, the sassy palm trees, and the glimmering Art Deco hotels make Miami a mecca for photographers. But there are no monuments here, no signature landmarks: Miami is a blank slate onto which one can project fantasies about wealth, sex, beauty, and romance. Miami indulges these desires, but endlessly defers gratification. Miami seduces photographers but always leaves them wanting more.

Almost too banal, and meaningless, for irony. One of the photographers shows a stiff sixtyish woman, her legs crossed, sitting on a purple bench, her young African American maid standing at a distance from her, holding a huge stupid-looking cat, both of them staring at the camera head-on, the floor marble. I hear the black population of Miami is about 20 percent and there is no power base. There is not one black model in the magazine—the worst ad possible, in this context, shows a "large private estate" along the intracoastal waterway "with elegant common rooms of great scale," "a very important lakefront statement," for only $36,500,000. There is a colored photograph of the house, fronted with a large swimming pool and palm trees, and the photograph has a black frame around it—as if it were one of the works of art on display at Art/Basel. I guess it is. There are also hugely expensive apartments for sale in NYC and ads by museums in other cities, Boston, LA, DC. There is one ad that states "To break the rules, you must first master them." It's a Swiss watch, and apparently the rule it broke was "to treat steel not as a building material but as a precious metal." The language is hideous and the big lie is underneath. Nor can I tell if the watch sells for nineteen dollars or five thousand, since filthy lucre is never mentioned. After all, though you would put a price tag on a de Kooning, you certainly wouldn't on such a watch, "now expressed in 41mm diameter, from avant-garde to icon," whatever that means.

I am particularly attracted to a full-bodied voluptuous nude sitting on a red background, her hands supporting her torso, a redder towel lying across her privates, her breasts gorgeous and a huge yellow rose, instead of a head, to top it off. It's called "Technician of the Sacred" (from Rothenberg) and is by one Linder, with the date of 2012 (with no apologies to Jerome). I guess it's a photo, since it doesn't seem like an ad for anything. On the reverse side (the next page) is a short article about the Davidoff cigar company, which has a walk-in humidor and an expert cigar roller in Davidoff's lush Caribbean-inspired hospitality area and information on the Davidoff Art Initiative, founded to support contemporary Caribbean artists in Berlin, Romania, China, and the Dominican Republic. To the left of that is an article about Jeff Koon's BMW Art Car and a photo of Warhol's 1979 BMW M1—on display in the BMW's VIP lounge. I'm sure Andy drew cars as a kid instead of learning fractions or memorizing the parts of speech, as I—and thousands of others—did. He was probably inspired by the Hupmobile. I was by the Packard. This is on page 226. The yellow rose is on page 265. Then there is a naked woman lying in a huge bed of flowers, her makeup very heavy (page 155), with an article about collectives or collaborative practice on the reverse (page 154). But on the reverse of a piece on the outsider artist at the Bass Museum, a "sprawling four-room display, titled ESL" (English as a second language), is the true piece of resistance, an ad for a store called Scoop NYC, showing a partially dressed model lying on the floor wearing 1950s nylons and a garter belt, holding in her right hand a large blossom against her (right) cheek and, with her left hand, touching herself. On the floor are some broken flowers and some books, including *The Picture of Dorian Gray*. The ad says Scoop NYC presents *Les Fleurs du mal,* Baudelaire's book, in small (salacious) print. Here, the greatest French book of poetry of the nineteenth century, associated with an undressed woman sort of masturbating on the terrazzo. I don't know if Charles would have approved. Either of the image or the forced connections. I don't know what Scoop NYC sells.

I can't blame Andy for all this. He died before the Beach was reguilded and the 960 historic buildings were gussied up and he went to New York—from Pittsburgh— to draw shoes for I. B. Miller and fell into a hole. He probably wore high heels at night. His best movie was about a social worker with a foot fetish. He was one of the two Andys. I suspect his father worked for the other. If there weren't already a South Beach, he might have invented it. He would have been absolutely at home in the art scene here, and he would have loved Basel. What one or two others might call a degradation.

Hoarders

There was a piece that came out in the Sunday *Times*, in the middle of October 2015, about a seventysomething-year-old man—named George Bell—who died alone in his apartment and lay there, without anyone's knowledge, for a week or so until a neighbor smelling the deteriorating corpse called the police, who went into a familiar action regarding such deaths, trying to identify family, friends, heirs, and the long tedious process of such actions, what city offices are involved, how much time it takes, and the like. I call it a piece but it is more an elegy, an essay, a meditation on such deaths—fifty thousand a year, the article says, in New York City alone, and the particulars of this person's dying, this person named George Bell, and what was done in his case.

After he was positively identified, and after talking to his neighbors and looking through the drawers of desks and dressers to ascertain his habits and look for his connections, a general picture was established. He wasn't married, had no children, was a hoarder, a loner, never admitted anyone to his apartment and even hung a heavy curtain at the entrance to his door, and had very little memorabilia. He bought six or even ten of everything, carpet cleaners, large bottles of Pepsi Lite, pencil sharpeners, and though the apartment had a bedroom, it was so clogged that he slept on a small daybed in the living room. He almost got married—as a young man—and even bought a suit, but after the breakup he abandoned the idea, though in a will he left most of his money to his old fiancée, who was—it turned out—already dead herself, so the money went to her nieces, whom George never knew, not even their names. He did have a car and every day moved it from one side of the street to the other, as you do in New York City. He was a very large man, 350 pounds, and had buddies whom he drank with at a local bar, but they all ascertained that though he was the life of the party, there was no intimacy, no personal things he admitted, and no one had visited him at home. He didn't cook but bought takeout, and since he had a ravenous appetite he was ashamed to go to restaurants for he would have to order at least three entrees. He had worked as a mover, lifting furniture and boxes, but after damaging his back he was on government assistance and didn't work anymore.

Though the piece in the *Times* wasn't on George Bell alone but on all those men and women who die alone, without friends and family. One woman, also a hoarder—but extreme—when she died, alone, she died standing up for there was no room on the floor for her to fall down and lie there. There must have been other hideous or unbearable details, and pets may have starved; and vermin may have gotten wind of the situation, oh most literally. Naturally, when you're ninety, as I am, you might worry; you probably do at sixty if you're living alone. And your near and dear—since they're mostly in their fifth decade—are still immortal, and immortals probably don't think of death that often. If they do in the abstract, or theoretically, it's a philosophical, not a personal, issue. Anaxagoras or some other Sicilian has got their back. My mother died at ninety-three, when I was sixty-eight and immortal, the way I describe it. I was the only one she had, and though she refused assisted living and was very difficult, I should have protected her more. There were things I could have done to reduce the anxiety she must have had, though she did have a community of sorts and would not have died totally alone. By contrast, I am living with a much younger woman who seldom leaves me alone and, if she does, then telephones me to make sure I'm all right. For which I feel guilty, burdening her. I sometimes think I should sell my house in Lambertville and give the proceeds to my children, get rid of my library and my furniture, add my remaining boxes of papers to my archives at the University of Pittsburgh, and find one and a half rooms by some water somewhere. But I live in NYC in a beautiful apartment, with a woman I love, and my doctors are nearby, and colleges in the city provide me with interns to help me, and I am still in the middle of a busy writing and social life. Most of all, I am limited in my walking and grow lonely quickly and am not like my Chinese cousins, ready for a hermit's life. My will and my last wishes are in a large envelope in a drawer beside my bed in Lambertville. And near and dear know where the envelope(s) are and what information it contains, and I have more or less decided to be buried in Mt. Hope Cemetery on a hill in Lambertville in the tiny Jewish sections, not in the Bronx and not in Pittsburgh with my sister and grandparents in a crowded Poland and not in the tropics with my mother and father. I am already planning another book of poems, *Galaxy Love* (the one after *Divine Nothingness*), which will probably be printed and released in about a year, plus the one after that, which already contains thirty or so poems and whose shape I am thinking about or at least waiting for the words and music to come to me since we poets control our writing destiny much less than we think we do.

I am reading the poems of C. K. Williams in his very last book, *Collected Later Poems*, sent to Anne Marie and me with a note—unsigned—that read in part: Charlie wanted you to have this. Charlie died a month or so ago from a blood cancer. We were in touch with him and Catherine constantly, brought them food, ate with them in restaurants, and tried to lift his spirits. He was losing a pound a day, was a virtual skeleton, and couldn't climb the steps in his house in Hopewell. He went constantly to the hospital in nearby Princeton, caught pneumonia, had blood transfusions, and was administered chemotherapy, which absolutely exhausted him. They finally gave up and invited hospice in. The poems, all of which I had read in the various volumes when they appeared, are deeply moving, original, and brilliant. The book is not near me now, but I am remembering two poems, one called "The Dress," about the mothers of his youth wearing shapeless "house dresses" as they went through their busy days, and the other called "Bialystok or Lodz," about his ancestors in Eastern Europe and how a great-grandfather, or great-

great, who owned a tavern, was murdered by a "berserk Cossack" in a disagreement, maybe about a bill, maybe about Jesus. There is also a more or less "private" poem about disagreements with Harold Brodkey, a former friend of Charlie's, and a rather famous writer twenty-five or so years ago. Its subject is really about dispute among artists and is not that private a poem, I see now. Charlie was a decade younger than me and it was too soon for him to go. He was the conscience of his generation and kept to his mode through thick and thin, approval and disapproval. In my view he is a great poet. He was kind, extremely generous, and had the withering voice of a prophet. I will miss him, as I miss Phil Levine and Galway Kinnell, as I grieve over the condition of William Merwin and Robert Bly. My generation, those born in the mid- to late twenties, has, at most, three or four left. We are antiques already to the new generations, who fill our journals and do the shouting.

It is conceivable that I'll die alone for I am *de temps en temps* by myself, but I'll not rot, whether in bed or on the floor. Nor do I feel a connection to the rotters and hoarders who seem to retire from the world when they reach their late sixties or early seventies. And I don't hang out in bars with the boys. I could think of nothing more boring, maybe being in solitary confinement, or at church. I probably won't move into my house in Lambertville, much as I love it, and I won't redo the first floor so I don't have to climb steps—and I don't think I'll buy a one-and-a-half- or two-roomer near a body of water to define my life more purely, for most of what I love is here. The arc of each of our lives is different. Mine is as it is and, like the hummingbird, *je ne regrette rien.* I wasn't lost on the wayside—I remade it, even with more weeds. As Bishop Beck said when I was a boy looking up at the chorus of blue-clad saints on Wylie Avenue playing their violins and singing their spirituals: "God bless Rosie Rosewell" and "God bless Eleanor Roosevelt" and "God bless Mayor Scully," who couldn't recite a fiery poem of his father's the way Roz Baraka did the other night in Newark, the number-one reader of poetry of all the mayors of America, where Amina, his mother, and I sang together and hugged and kissed each other. "Bless the fallen pears and apples in two of my former backyards" and "bless baby's breath, both human and flowery" and Rebecca and Dylan and Julia and Alana Rose and "bless the thirsty wrens and the orangutans." Most of all the orangutans.

Books of the Dead

I suppose you end a book when you have nothing more to say, which is only another way of saying you are done with that particular obsession—or narrative or problem. For a book is, after all, a *problem* and it's also problematic; think of *Finnegan's Wake*, which is problematic because of its post- or pre-intelligible language, the way the book is popularly perceived. It is for that reason that probably very few people actually read it, choosing—if anything— to deal with it by hearsay, or by looking over a (very) few pages. As I've said before, I loved the book, read it from cover to cover while holed up in an empty apartment for a week, ate from time to time, and did one-handed push-ups while standing upside-down against a wall. I related to the language, the cyclical philosophy, the specific narrative, and the latent grief. It was Joyce's plan, we are told, to write a short, simple book after the *Wake* in order to complete the cycle—but he died. Perhaps he intended to go in the direction of his secretary and assistant, Samuel Beckett. At least as far as the language, if not the vision. Joyce was always one step ahead of his critics.

As far as *this* book, I'm not sure what it achieved. I certainly got lost in the details, I let my pen and the mere accidents of my life take over—to a smaller or larger degree. The overriding theme was death; death itself, plus *my* death, plus the end of a journey, though that sounds banal. It is a comedy, and for two reasons—one because the writing is, if anything, comedic, and two, no one dies during the writing. At least no one of immediate importance. It took me a lifetime to learn that I was a comic writer—as I see "comic" and as I've written about it, including in this book. So, my own death—or my coming death—is comic? Well, it's not tragic. I insist on that!

If it's a book about death, it's concerned as much about the after-life as it is concerned about the life, except that the life, what we call this dreamtime, is itself very much concerned both with the after-life and with the afterlife, two more or less separate things. Many of my friends, Christian, atheist, agnostic, ask me what the Jewish view of the afterlife is, as if we Jews were all expected to answer on the same note and to believe as one, we arguers, each with his or her own book. When I tell my questioner (who sits so sly) that the chief rabbi of Canada is—or, if he's dead, was—an atheist, and that my uncle George (whose name was actually Joseph) wouldn't allow the doctors to cut off his foot because he didn't want to be resurrected as a cripple, and that they were both good Jews and considered as such by all except the most black-clad of us, the questioner nods his (or her) head, but in disbelief.

Jews are either consumed by fire or left to rot in a box, like everybody else. So much for the after-life. As for the afterlife, the answer is "Well! Jack Benny's well!" If you want to know what Jews believed in at the time of Jesus, one is a little tempted to say that the Christian heaven was the Jewish heaven, lock and stock, although you'd have to except the Sadducees, for it was confined to the Pharisees, Jesus's party. But, for God's sake, Jews don't—or shouldn't—get credit for "heaven" (though they have something of a claim for heaven on earth) since all religions, all cultures, have a version of it. And it seems always to be a continuation of the favorite earthly activity, whether it be killing birds or reading books. I read somewhere that belief in transmigration was a common thing among medieval mystics of the Hebrew persuasion. Maybe they got sick of being murdered by Crusaders on their way to Jerusalem and wanted to become spiders (or wasps or mosquitoes) so they could take revenge. There are huge numbers of Jewish Buddhists (Jubus) in the U.S. and Canada. I heard a statistic that two-thirds of the Buddhists in California are Jews. Maybe they are particularly attracted to "nothingness," which is an ancient Jewish term. I own a book entitled *Zen and Hasidism*, which I am reading through for the third time maybe. It contains essays by Martin Buber, Zalman Schechter, Jeri Langer, Jacob Yaroh Teshima, Gary Snyder, and many others. I used to half-believe in the similarity of the two, but there is too much difference to link them together, though they both do contain a striving for naught. But I would not accuse the Hasids of non-attachment. Unless spitting at Buddha on the road or bowing down to worship God are one and the same thing. There are common strains in all the religions, and if Christianity and Judaism were not at such loggerheads, and if you came to them fresh, say without a knowledge of history, it would be interesting to connect them. Why is it so hard for the Piuses to understand that the cross is an aversion to Jews? And an insult when it is thrust in our faces. The Jewish vampire, when a cross (preferably silver) is held above the poor victim, he—the vampire—responds (in Yiddish) *"Soll ihr*

Gornisht Helfen!" (It won't do you a damn bit of good) or just "up yours, man."

I identified once with the Chinese poet-bureaucrat who, when he reached old age (sixty!) left everybody, his wife, children, home, brushes, to walk into the mountains and take up a solitary life, in a hut maybe, with a beggar's pot, maybe with a fishing pole. I am thinking that now as I accept old age, and before I enter the state of "extreme old age," I had better take off for a mountain while I can still think—and walk—straight. My only problem is my deep connections on the one hand and my bad nerve endings on the other. Is there a place for me, a monastery, an art-ist's retreat, a mother-in-law's house? Is it in Costa Rica, Vermont, the Outer Banks, Atlantic City? Could I leave Anne Marie, my grandchildren, my books? Isn't it a shame that Harry Schwartz and Vivian Gornick weren't able to establish apartments for elder artists in New York? But would I want to be confined to such a place? Just imagine a retirement home for poets, like the ones for musicians or actors. There would be such violence, not what an elder needs, or wants. Is there a hotel somewhere, in the Catskills, the Alleghenies, Philadelphia? Am I barking up a dead tree?

Whatever I might do, I have to say goodbye to Sylvia. She died and was buried in the Jewish cemetery in Carrick, a neighborhood in Pittsburgh. I wrote once about that cemetery as a crowded small city, on a hill, Eastern European Jewish names, as well as American versions, abounding. I would be willing to don a prayer shawl and sway endlessly if I thought there was an Elysium and she was in it. I would buy such a broad-brimmed hat that Jewish swallows could build their clay nests under its folds. Did she protect me in this long life? I think of my differing versions of her life—had she lived—and I take up the thought again. How difficult for a beautiful Jewish girl, born in the earliest days of 1924, would life have been? How difficult in particular would it have been, with the parents she had, their fears, naïveté, ignorance, evasion, sentimentality, and soul-stifling conventionality. Three times as hard as for me. Unless she joined in their make-believe world. Though I don't think she would have. Could we not talk once and question each other over what might have been? Can shades kiss? Should I show her what I'm writing or should I read her a poem? I think I would want to hide my luck so her burden wouldn't be heavier. But wouldn't she have arrived at another place—for we aren't Greeks who long to taste of the life once more and exist for that memory. Could I tell her that she had been my muse—always? Couldn't I find a different word?

But don't you talk to the dead, or their spirits, as Aeneas did, and Odysseus, as we do in dreams? Does someone guide us in their boat? Is it like the ferry in New London, or is it a large rowboat? Does it have a motor? Is there a special coin, some learned doves? Would I want to talk to *my* father as Aeneas did with his, is there an old friend, a dead poet, a relative, a teacher, to talk to in Elysium? What is the tree called in New Jersey that the Golden Bough hangs from? Is it also an ilex? How old would *my* Sybil be? Is my father's shade also like thin air? Is the Mullica River the River of Forgetfulness, or is it the Batsto? Do we leave by the ivory gate also?

It's a kind of strange obsession, talking, communicating, with the dead. It may be most prevalent in "nonbelieving" cultures like ours. I vaguely remember my parents trying to reach Sylvia and my mother taking the lead. We see it on TV and in movies, we read about it. My favorite incident is in Yeats's play *Words Upon the Windowpane* where there is a séance taking place in the very house in Dublin where Jonathan Swift lived. The medium—as I remember—was not a very literate person, and the table was peopled mostly with New Scoffers. Suddenly, with the room lit only by flickering candles and the secularists holding hands, comes a deep voice from the medium, Swift's voice, repeating the words he had incised in the window glass in the hallway going upstairs, "Perish the day on which I was born," Swift's voice, and Job's, a great play that I have dreamed for years of producing. But the dead go to visit—or revisit—us, they come back but they have absolutely nothing to say about the place they reside in. It's almost as if they're not interested, or we're not interested. The single most valuable thing they could bear witness to, those ghosts. A complicated con.

There is a book I read once, or looked through, of famous deaths. Famous last words. Oscar Wilde's, "That wallpaper has to go," or Henry James's, "At last, the great good thing." It may have been in that book where I read of William James's last words and his death. He is emeritus, at his desk at Harvard, when the black angel arrives. And he writes down, maybe on the blotter, maybe on an envelope, "What conclusions can we make? What can we conclude in regard to . . . ?" He, psychologist, philosopher, teacher, mystic, physician, invalid, theosophist, adventurer, linguist, great soul, trying to arrive at "conclusions," as a therapist, say in Philadelphia, might "seek closure." Yet the biographers—of all things—say that he died at his summer home in Chocorua, of heart failure. I guess hard by Mt. Chocorua, on top of which I wrote my second or third bad poem when I was sixteen or seventeen.

Diane Freund, whom I talked to on the phone thirty to forty minutes before she died, two or three years ago, succumbed to brain cancer after the original breast cancer metastasized. I must say that she seemed calm and alert, in spite of her impending death and the drugs she must have been taking. We talked for ten or fifteen minutes. It was more than a bit eerie, for she told me that her agent had just sold her second novel to a publisher, as if she had forgotten for a minute where she was and what was happening. She had a foot, so to speak, in both worlds. Or she had either not made the transference or had—temporarily—returned. I am haunted by this and always will be. Death and life interacting. Was there a time when it was easier? Will that time return? Will the most important single event in our lives become less terrifying? Where will I be? Or how?

Maybe I should go back to *The Egyptian Book of the Dead*. Is the title, *Book of Emerging Forth into the Light*, an ancient statement about the brilliant light that the dead—who come back—see when they leave this life, when they "set forth," as Dylan Thomas said in a birthday poem? Since the earliest "entries" were on the walls of pyramids and were for the sake of the dead pharaoh (and his wife), their journey into the next world, aided by incantations, spells, and magic, where they would finally sit beside the gods, whether in the blue sky above or the black underworld below. After a while high officials were granted the right, but I don't think farmers or butchers. Maybe poets. As in all cultures, if you had enough gelt you could reach the gods easily. You could hire a scribe to describe *your* journey on papyrus and encase it in your coffin. Spells were, so to speak, chapters in a book. The word "ra," which began most spells, could also mean "mouth," "speech," "utterance," or "incantation." Some (spells) give the dead person knowledge in—and of—the afterlife, some were to protect the dead from harm and to guide him through obstacles and—of course—to help him, or her, deal with judgment. Words themselves had magical powers, whether spoken or written, and full use was made of amulets, which were wound into the wrappings of the mummy, and, as always, knowing the name of something gave you power over it. The funerary rituals were all consumed with the preservation of the dead, from the most mundane, such as providing food and water, to the saying of the name of the dead person in order to maintain his continued existence.

The dead person was taken into the presence of Osiris and even helped the god in his own struggles, since he—the dead one—became a quasi-deity himself. The dead might live in the Field of Reeds, a paradisiac likeness of the real world, a lush version of the world they had lived in. Of course the dead had to overcome many obstacles, travel through gates and caverns and encounter ferocious creatures, who had to be pacified by the spells. The ultimate thing was the judgment, as in all religions. Here the heart was weighed—against an ostrich feather—in order to ascertain the dead person's freedom from committing any sins, from an official list of forty-two. If the dead were actually free of sin or if he could recite the appropriate spell, he was free to progress into the afterlife, according to the judgment of Osiris. It is a little different from the Last Judgment or the Book of Life, but it was workable in its way.

The Tibetan Book of the Dead, compared to the Egyptian seems, if less pragmatic, then more spiritual, or complicated. I discovered the most recent version, written in 2005, only a little while ago in 2016. It was described—on the cover—as the "first complete translation," and there is an introductory commentary by the Dalai Lama as well as other introductions, and it is 535 pages long. The other two (versions) are by Stephen Hodges, 1999, and the more famous W. Y. Evans-Wentz, 1927. It is this version that had such a profound effect on the Beats, druggies, and chanters of the late 1950s and early 1960s, Burroughs, Leary, Ginsberg, who, according to Brion Gysin in his novel *The Last Museum*, where the devotees are depicted as chanting in the streets, their heads shaven like Tibetan monks and wearing orange robes, were "earnestly passing around a copy of the Bardo Thodol, *The Tibetan Book of the Dead*, handwritten on dried banana leaves." Which puts the most important Tibetan book in a comic, even ridiculous, light and constitutes a kind of colonialism little better than that of the Chinese. It was Evans-Wentz who coined the title *The Tibetan Book of the Dead*, which is called, in Tibetan, *The Great Liberation by Hearing in the Intermediate States*. The Dalai Lama kept Evans-Wentz's title, since it was well known, in English, by that name.

In many ways *The Tibetan Book of the Dead* is the absolute opposite of the Egyptian. It is committed not to maintaining and protecting every detail from this life but rather to a complete liberation from it, you might say an escape (from it). Simply put, it is a guide for the dead (or dying) during the state between death and either liberation or rebirth. It is read aloud either to the dying or to the corpse itself so that he/she can attain escape from the cycle of rebirth.

Once awareness is freed from the body it needs help for enlightenment and liberation to occur. This happens through the reading of, and listening to, what are called Bardos. In the new book they are called intermediate or transitional states. The first Bardo—or intermediate— comes at the time of death itself. It is called the Clear Light of the Ultimate Reality, that famous light again. It is possible that he or she will remain in this clear light forever, thus achieving complete liberation, but most souls are pulled down by their ignorance or inattention. Unlike *The Egyptian Book of the Dead* it is liberation for anyone, from any class. The rest of the intermediate states are progressions. The dead one—his or her soul really— encounters first the "peaceful deities," one each for seven days, (according to Evans-Wentz). Then the wrathful deities for twelve (sometimes fourteen) days, if the soul is not liberated during the progression. The entire process takes forty-nine days, whatever a "day" is. Always the purpose is not to be attached, angry, envious, aggressive, contentious. The dead (or dying) person is at an advantage if they are familiar with the Bardos. Usually either a Lama or a learned or a close friend reads or recites them. However, both the peaceful and wrathful deities exist only in the mind of the dead or dying person, so however terrifying they might seem they are really only illusory. Projections.

My problem, with all these versions, is the literalness, the abstract language, the matter-of-factness of miraculous events, and the very lack of doubt, as if we were measuring the distance between two nearby towns and not delving into pure mystery—as well as the invisible. Look at this sentence: "A quiet and pleasant room with some religious symbols is very helpful." This, when we're talking about eternity, or "on the third day the primal form of the element earth will shine forth as a yellow light," or (from the "new" book) "[On the first day of the intermediate state of reality], all space will arise as a blue light. At this time . . . the transcendent lord Vairocana will dawn before you, his body white in colour, seated on a lion throne, holding in his [right] hand an eight-spoked wheel and embraced by his consort. A blue luminosity, radiant and clear, bright and dazzling, [indicative of] the pristine cognition of reality's expanse . . . will shine piercingly before you." And if there is a body, the guide should read the Great Liberation through Hearing three or seven times in a whisper, close to the ears of the deceased (who hopefully still has his or her hearing). And if there is no (dead) body present, the person reading the text should sit on the bed or a chair that belonged to the deceased person, speak with sincerity, and draw the spirit of the deceased to him. It is helpful, in this case, to have a portrait of the deceased present.

There is a Last Judgment even in Evans-Wentz and an explicit rendering of a cloth painting containing the punishment and/or reward after dying, when the Lord of Death consorts with the Mirror of Karma. Once again, as in *The Egyptian Book of the Dead*, there is a scale, not this time with a feather but with white and black pebbles on the weights, for the good and evil deeds. Lying will count for nothing, "for every good and evil act is reflected" in the mirror. The Lord of Death (in Evans-Wentz) has a headdress adorned with human skulls. There is a little white god and little black god to empty the pebbles from sacks. As in all Last Judgments, there are daemons of all sorts, furies, guides, paths for the guides, swords, whips, saws, torture tables, the dead standing in line, mean sub-gods, vicious animals, headless corpses, boiling water, neck-ropes, extruded intestines, hearts, livers, and the like, cups of blood, hacking, pieces of flesh, gnawed bones, animal-headed humans, and misery, fear, awe, terror, and emptiness, but it is all hallucinatory and an illusion. And the Clear Light can come in a second. Redemption—en-lightenment—is pictured on the upper end of the cloth painting, the top, but not too vividly since torture and punishment are always more interesting, as far as imagery is concerned, whether Tibetan or Christian.

The Book has always been the Jewish way, at least from the days of the rabbis on, post-Temple, as it were. We are told that the angel of death carries the book with him and writes down names or erases them, constantly. He goes by many names, Samuel, Saurmail, Azrael, Suriel, Sauriel, Coolidge, Hoover, Charlemagne, Greenberg. The Muslims also have a grand usher, a kind of judge, who also has a great book, not unlike the Jewish book for they derived it from the Jews. The Christian judge, be he Jesus or one of the Billies, doesn't have a book—or a feather, or black and white pebbles, but there must be something recognized as physical, for a judge requires evidence. He, she, can't remember everything. Henry Miller (noted else-where) made fun of an adult male who couldn't stop read-ing from his book even when he crossed the street, one of Miller's anti-Semitic slurs—for the man was a Jew. Of course Miller was a deep reader himself, but I guess only a Jew is foolish enough to cross a street in New York with his eyes in a book. Many preadolescent girls, often in the backseat of cars on long voyages, read endlessly, as much as anything else to remove themselves from the boring antics of their brothers and the banalities of their parents. Any woman reading this who was once such a girl please raise your left hand. We humans are obsessed with judgments and the courtrooms and films where it is acted out. And lawyers and judges who are called "your honor" and in some countries wear wigs. A large portion of our "shows" on TV take place in courtrooms. And I venture to say that underneath the particulars of the trials is the mythical battle between good and evil, the righteous and the sinner. Myself, I tend to forgive myself more and more my own peccadillos, or even my dillos, my more questionable feelings and acts, those of the black pebbles. I don't know if forgiving yourself makes you a judge and if you thenceforth have to address yourself as "your honor." I am content if my own books, poetry and prose, contain all that I'm to be judged by. There is certainly more than enough of my person in there. Though I can't personally be trusted as a true judge. But then neither can a critic for he—or she—donned her own critical hat with no one's blessing. So be it.

What strikes me in all cases—Buddhist, Muslim, Jewish—is that what is called liberation or reward or redemption, in whatever form it takes, is based, ultimately, on our actions toward others, be they family members or strangers, in what I embarrassingly call "this life." Thomas Eliot, in one of his Fascist rants, bans "free-thinking Jews" from his proposed "Anglo-Saxon" society, by which he probably means more or less nonobservant or secular Jews, but less observant Christians I guess are all right since it is basically a matter of culture, not religion, per se. Muslims are not even considered, let alone Buddhists. Nor does he mention Orthodox Jews. The Last Judgment is, to secularists, not a single act but an ongoing process, and the "judge" is probably implicit, more or less nonexistent, or like the judge—certainly that—in Kafka's *Trial*, there and not there simultaneously. I, personally, may get a little hysterical *de temps en temps,* but my God leans toward Spinoza's, as I understand him, and doesn't speak English or have a beard (or even a head). Like most post-Nietzscheans, I tend to call (her) "nothingness" and am pleased that Talmudic Jews call (him) "the name." And I don't think the name (Hashem) puts me in the dock, puts on his wire-rims, and looks at what is in the Book. I do my things because I have to, because they need to be done, because to overlook them would be stupid, "counterproductive," as we once said. Because Hashem and I love each other.

A lovely African American man said God bless you to me in a Southern restaurant on 110th Street earlier this evening. Anne Marie and I both had fried chicken but with different sides. I had potato salad and collard greens. A little bit of heaven. Well, heaven enough for me. I only wish my grandchildren were there with me.

The End

Let me say that I'm glad I suffered this life, though I know it sounds presumptuous and even foolish to say it. And I was blessed—though what I say is I was lucky. Phil Levine, when he was dying, said to me that he had a good life and he was ready to go. Charlie Williams, who died a year later, never stopped struggling though I am sure thought long and hard and talked to his dear ones. Those of us who survive somewhat longer, what are we to say, that we had two more books in us? Two more great books? I loved Charlie dearly and miss him, but it is not all about counting books. If you are going on ninety-one you know some things a little more differently than when you were going on sixty-one. And if your friends, out of kindness, say you look ten years younger—or twenty—thank them, kiss them, but know thyself. One of the sayings I like from the Greek. Artists are indeed all lucky if they have books or openings or contracts for a year hence and thence for they can, in a way, live in the future. They can imagine themselves still alive in the hence and thence, certainly in the hence. I have written some last testaments in the last few years, and where I stand (or sit or lie) is pretty clear, though you must perforce keep a little back—even to yourself—for who the hell are you (on the right-hand silver knob) to comb your white beard with your thin fingers and raise your right eyebrow? How about "alas poor Dickinson or Charlemagne or Picasso"? Or "alas poor Mayfly"? And Charlie does, as it turns out, have two more books, *The Collected Later*, and a new one—out in a few months.

And what was I? A little dust that sang too much? A miracle to beat all others? What is a sea of reeds opening up compared to that? Or curing a few very sick people (without a license, mind you)?

How many times do we have to repeat that Yehoshua—and the other prophets—will have their mouths sewn shut if they don't shut up about justice mercy humility and the other crap. I love Marlowe for what he said about caterpillars and Howard Zinn for what he said about America. May he (Yehoshua) sneeze on the literalists; and turn all oppressors of any stripe into dust balls, and save Coney Island, Miami Shores, and the Marshals from what coal and oil is doing; commodities we call them.

Death Poems

Though there is something too peaceful about it, too Buddhistic, the feeling we are left here at the end. Shiva is over for the night, we are putting our shoes on over our socks, some black, some with clocks, some white and athletic, and we are getting ready to get up from our chairs (or boxes) and drive down—in second gear—to the Second Avenue Deli and have a plate full of white fish or some lox and cream cheese and be almost murmurous, like birds utterly worn out from a daytime of extreme whistling, and peter down as the light leaves us, in late August where we will have to be retrieving some thick wool blankets from the blanket box, or at least a heavier sheet than usual, maybe something netted or cottony.

Is it for this reason—yes, it is—that I am also retrieving a few poems about the awful subject, of the thousands there are, what occurs to me in a few seconds in our apartment with very few books as yet, certainly not one on death poems, an anthology I don't yet have. There must be such an anthology, maybe several. They are called *Death and Dying*, *The Bitter End*, or just *Endless.*

There is a case to be made that all lyric poems are about death, but I am going to skip that. I'm thinking of Kenneth Fearing, Dickinson, Cummings, Ginsberg, Neruda, Dylan Thomas, Celan. Whitman and Levis. In the next few seconds twelve others occur, but I am not going to do the anthology. Mark Strand, Goethe, C. K., etc. Neruda has many death poems, "Irresistible death . . . ," which ends "dying of my own death" (*Muriendo de mi propia muerte*), or "Death Alone," where death is personified as "waiting dressed as an admiral" (*vestida de almirante*), which I compare (in tone and structure) to Larry Levis's marvelous *La Strada* ("In the Darkening Trapeze"): "and I guess / Death will blow his little fucking trumpet." In context, overwhelmingly moving.

Or Paul Celan's "Death Fugue" ("Death is a master from Germany") or Dylan Thomas's "Do not go gentle into that good night" or his "And death shall have no dominion" ("Dead men naked they shall be one / with the man in the moon and the west moon") or Cummings's "And what i want to know is / how do you like your blueeyed boy Mr. Death." From "Buffalo Bill's defunct . . ." Or Kenneth Fearing's "Dirge,"

and biff got married and bam had children and oof got
 fired,
zowie did he live and zowie did he die,
With who the hell are you at the corner of his casket, and
 where the hell we going on the right-hand silver knob,
 and who
the hell cares walking second from the end with an
 American Beauty wreath from why the hell not,
Very much missed by the circulation staff of the *New
 York Evening Post*; deeply, deeply mourned by the
 B.M.T.,
Wham, Mr. Roosevelt; pow, Sears Roebuck; awk, big
 dipper; bop, summer rain;
Bong, Mr., bong, Mr., bong, Mr., bong.

Or, above all, Whitman:

Has any one supposed it lucky to be born?
I hasten to inform him or her, it is just as lucky to die,
 and I know it.

Or

This grass is very dark to be from the white heads of old
 mothers,
Darker than the colorless beards of old men,

Dark to come from under the faint red roofs of mouths.

And Dickinson:

Because I could not stop for Death —
He kindly stopped for me —
I heard a fly buzz — when I died —

Ginsberg's "Kaddish" is really not a death poem; for that matter Kaddish itself is not about the dead, but praise—in Aramaic—for Hashem, variously called Adonoi, Jehovah, God, and Yahwah. Allen gave me a drawing that Naomi, his mother, did while in a mental institution.

I am looking over Rebecca Solnit's *Hope in the Dark,* a *Nation* book published in 2004, which I looked over once before—thoroughly—eight or nine years ago. Great on the Zapatistas. My glorious time in San Cristóbel twenty-five years ago. Time a Florida Amerindian family parked their truck in front of my old house on the Delaware River on old 611 south of Easton, Pennsylvania, and asked if they could fish on my land—or *from* my land. They caught some bass and I invited them into my house to make their supper. Their tribe was—they told me—still at war with the U.S., but we called a truce and ate together. I think my wife and children were there. I had supper while I was sleeping last night with someone who was a cross between Franz Kafka and Martin Buber. Latkes and sour cream. Goes well with bass. Goodnight, Irene.

GERALD STERN's recent books of poetry are *Divine Nothingness, In Beauty Bright, Early Collected Poems, 1965–1992, Save the Last Dance, Everything Is Burning, American Sonnets, Last Blue, This Time: New and Selected Poems*, which won the National Book Award, *Odd Mercy*, and *Bread without Sugar*. His essay collections *What I Can't Bear Losing* and *Stealing History* are available from Trinity University Press. His honors include the Ruth Lilly Prize, four National Endowment for the Arts grants, the American Academy of Arts and Letters Award of Merit for Poetry, the *Paris Review*'s Bernard F. Conners Award, the Pennsylvania Governor's Award for Excellence in the Arts, and fellowships from the Academy of American Poets, the Guggenheim Foundation, and the Pennsylvania Council on the Arts. In 2005 Stern received the Wallace Stevens Award for mastery in the art of poetry, the National Jewish Book Award for poetry, and, in 2013, the

Frost Medal from the Poetry Society of America. He has been a chancellor of the Academy of American Poets and for many years a teacher at the University of Iowa Writers' Workshop. Stern lives in Lambertville, New Jersey, and New York City.